DEDICATION

This book is dedicated to the Hawaiian people and to the aloha spirit. May they both endure.

HIKING OAHU

The Capital Isle

Robert Smith

Wilderness Press
BERKELEY

Maps by Kevin G. Chard
Cover photo by the author
Design by Thomas Winnett

Library of Congress Card Catalog Number 77-88641
International Standard Book Number 911824-63-4

Manufactured in the United States

Published by Wilderness Press
            2440 Bancroft Way
            Berkeley, California 94704

ACKNOWLEDGEMENTS

Many people made significant contributions to this book. Thanks to Bill Crane for his companionship on many of the hikes and for his knowledge and helpful suggestions. Thanks also to Fred Samia, who assisted by reading the manuscript. I am indebted to Louis Mellencamp, who contributed professional advice and assistance on the photos included in this volume. A special mahalo to Nancy, my wife, for typing the manuscript.

Photo credits

Robert Smith: pages 19, 27, 31, 41, 50, 55, 57, 61, 69, 89, 91, 95, 98, 102, 106
Thomas Winnett: pages ii, 7, 25, 35, 37, 74
Bob Immler: page viii

Contents

Northern Oahu shore

Part I: Introduction

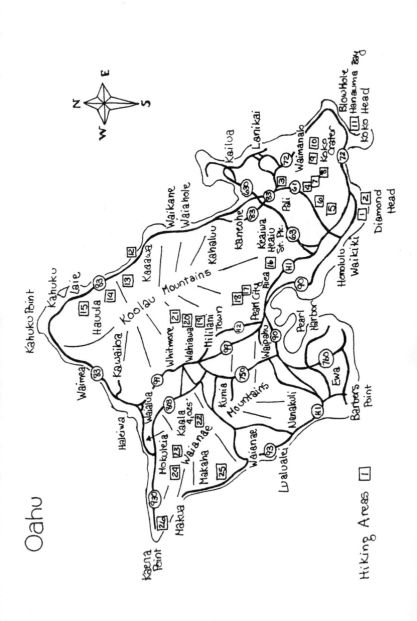

Oahu

Hiking Areas [I]

The Island

Take a walk along Waikiki Beach any time of the day, any time of the year, and you will understand why this, the third largest of the Hawaiian Islands, is called Oahu, "the gathering place": Everyone is here—Japanese, Chinese, Filipinos, Blacks, Samoans, Germans, Canadians, Australians and others.

What is it that brings people here from all over the world? Can it be the air temperature, which seldom varies by more than 10 degrees, with a year-round average of 75°F? Can it be the 80° water temperature at Waikiki Beach? Can it be the enchantment of precipitous cliffs and heavily overgrown valleys existing as backdrops to a city covered with asphalt and high-rise buildings? Can it be the fascinating blend of the multi-ethnic population? Can it be the life style in which individuality reigns supreme, and muumuus and cutoffs, oxfords and bare feet, tuxedoes and swimsuits intermingle in the restaurants and discotheques? Can it be the surf, the music, the sun-tanned bodies, the aloha spirit, the wild fruits, the hiking, the camping, the slow pace of life, the . . . . ?

The truth is that Waikiki, and Honolulu, are all of these things. The truth is that long before the first-time visitor arrives, Hawaii has transmitted its message via the plaudits of happy visitors, the media, and the Hawaii Visitors Bureau. The truth is that the first-time visitor has been primed for pleasure long before his jumbo 747 flies over Diamond Head and lands in Honolulu. For most people, there are no disappointments, and they return again and again.

Indeed, the crowds are sometimes so great that people spill off the sidewalk onto Kalakaua Avenue in order to get by casual strollers. Combine the 2-million-plus tourists who visit Oahu annually with the 705,000 permanent residents (over 80% of the state's population) and you have a lot of people on a rather small island.

Honolulu was not an original Hawaiian city. It was established by the followers of Captain Cook who, in search of anchorage, discovered this protected deep-water bay. Honolulu (lit., "protected bay") grew rapidly and was soon recognized as the trading and business center of the islands by King Kamehameha III. The official capital of the Kingdom of Hawaii was moved from Lahaina, Maui, to Honolulu in 1850. For the next 85 years, the southeast end of the city remained a swamp where taro was cultivated and ducks and other marsh birds roamed freely. However, in the past 40 years Waikiki has been dramatically altered from its humble beginnings to become one of the most recognized beaches in the world.

But there is more to Oahu than world-famous Waikiki, Diamond Head and Pearl Harbor. On the windward (east) side of the island are the Hawaiian communities of Hauula and Laie, where numerous valley hikes and beach camping, away from the crowds, awaits the outdoors person. The north shore of Oahu may well be the surfing capital of the world, with the Banzai Pipeline, Sunset Beach and Waimea Bay, but it is also the departure point for hikes to a number of peaks along the Waianae mountain range. And lastly, there are the central plains, where most of the island's pineapple and sugar cane are grown, and where the trailheads are located for hikes up to the Koolau mountain range for striking panoramas of the island.

The two mountain ranges and the island of Oahu were created by volcanic eruptions. Oahu took shape

as subsequent lava flows filled the area between the
ranges until the present 607 square miles remained.
In time, the Koolau mountain range on the east side
and the Waianae mountain range on the west side
were further sculpted by natural forces, so that both
have gently sloping parts and steep precipitous areas.

Although there are no hikes on Oahu to compare
to the Kalalau Trail on Kauai, the trails in Haleakala
Crater on Maui or the Mauna Loa Trail to the 13,680-
foot summit on Hawaii, there are trails to excite and
to challenge the hiker. The Dupont Trail to Mt.
Kaala, the highest point (4025 feet) on Oahu, is an
outstanding hike, and the hikes to Sacred Falls and
into Poamoho Valley are equal to any of the valley
hikes on the other islands.

Using This Book

While most of the hikes on Oahu are short-distance, part-day hikes, I have included a wide selection of trips from short, easy family walks to long, difficult hikes. Many of the hikes are on public lands where well-maintained trails direct the hiker. Other hikes are on private land—pineapple and sugar-cane holdings— and some are on military reservations. In spite of the time and effort required to secure permission from property owners, I have included these worthy hikes. For example, the Poamoho Ridge Trail (Hiking Area No. 21) is a noble hike, but it requires permission from the State Division of Forestry, the US Army, the Dole Pineapple Co. and the Wailua Sugar Company! I have not included areas from which hikers are forbidden by law (protected watershed) or where the terrain is dangerous and unsafe even though local people may boast of their adventures into these places. Each year numerous injuries and some fatalities occur where people have hiked in spite of the prohibition. For example, a prominent sign at the end of the Manoa Falls Trail (Hiking Area No. 7) warns hikers not to climb above the falls, where the terrain is brittle and treacherous. Nevertheless, numerous injuries, rescues, and even deaths have been recorded there in recent years. In the first nine months of 1977, four hikers died on Oahu! However, good judgment and a regard for the time-tested rules of hiking are good protection.

In order to ensure a safe and enjoyable experience and to protect the environment, remember:

1. Do not hike alone.
2. Many Hawaiian trails are wet and slippery, and the terrain is loose and brittle.
3. Contrary to popular belief, it is not possible to live off the land. Carry your own food.
4. Although some fruits are available, never eat or taste unknown fruits or plants.
5. Carry your own water or purify water from streams.
6. A tent with a rain fly ensures comfortable and dry nights.
7. Carry your trash out.
8. Bury personal waste away from streams.
9. Firewood in most places is not available or is too wet for use. Carry a stove for cooking.
10. Darkness begins right after sunset.

In planning a hike, the reader is advised to consult the Hiking Chart below in order to give due consideration to driving time, hiking time, and the clothing and supplies necessary. I have rated all the hikes and placed them in one of four categories. A "family" rated hike is for those who are looking for short, easy hikes. The "hardy family" classification requires a degree of effort and sound physical condition. Both the strenuous and the difficult hikes require a measure of endurance, since they are longer hikes and most of them involve a considerable gain in altitude. They also require good footwear and more equipment.

Obviously, hiking time varies from person to person, depending on such factors as pace and the extent to which one chooses to linger for lunch and to swim where pools exist. The time noted in the Hiking Chart is based on a leisurely pace. Trail distance is based either on an exact measurement or on an approximation with the aid of a topographic map.

Driving time and mileage cited are based on the posted speed limit and are measured from Waikiki.

Specific driving instructions precede each hike description.

The equipment noted on the Hiking Chart is minimal for hiking enjoyment. As a rule, however, I always carry water, food and a first-aid kit. Although the choice between tennis shoes and hiking boots is listed in some cases as optional, I prefer hiking boots in most cases. Obviously, your feet are an important consideration in hiking since it is common, on an island that has experienced extensive volcanic activity, to have volcanic ash or rock underfoot. Usually, shorts or long pants are optional, except where the brush is thick or when the weather requires warmer clothing.

Drinking water is available from streams in many areas, but it should be boiled or treated, since cattle, pigs and goats may share the water supply. To avoid the chance of illness, carry one quart of water per person. In many areas, firewood is at a premium. A small, light, reliable backpacking stove is a convenience and a comfort if you plan to cook out.

Before each hike description you will find the hike rating, trail features, hiking distance and time, specific driving instructions, instructions for getting there by bus and introductory notes. On some hikes it is necessary to walk on private property. Information and addresses are provided so that you can secure permission in advance. Permission is usually readily granted either over the telephone or in person when you sign a liability waiver.

In the trail narrative I usually mention the flora and fauna to be seen along the way, especially the unusual and the unique, in an effort to add to your hiking enjoyment. But I don't mention everything, and you may wish to buy one of several guides to plants and animals of the islands, available at many stores. I recommend *Tropical Trees of Hawaii* and

Hawaii Blossoms both by Dorothy and Bob Hargreaves and *Hawaii's Birds* by the Hawaii Audubon Society.

Preceding each trail narrative is a map that will help you find the trailhead and to locate trail highlights. The maps show many features of the hikes as well as campsites.

The fine public transportation system on Oahu deserves a special note. Many visitors make the mistake of renting a car when "The Bus"—yes that's what it's called—is convenient, reliable, comfortable and inexpensive. The Bus makes regular stops at most places of interest on the island. Unquestionably, The Bus is the best bargain on Oahu. For 25¢ you can ride nearly 100 miles around the island: From Honolulu, The Bus travels along the east coast, passes across the north shore and returns through the central portion of Oahu to Honolulu. The system is so reliable that I have included instructions for taking The Bus to the trailheads.

Symmetrical young Norfolk Island pine

Hiking Chart

Column groups — Hike Rating: Family, Hardy Family, Strenuous, Difficult · Trail Time: Distance (miles) (L indicates loop), Time (hours), Gain in feet · From Waikiki: Miles, Time (hours) · Equipment: Raingear, Boots, Tennis Shoes, Carry Water, Take Food · Features: Swimming, Waterfalls, Views, Historical Sites, Fruits

No.	Hiking Chart	Family	Hardy Family	Strenuous	Difficult	Distance (miles) (L=loop)	Time (hrs)	Gain in feet	Miles	Time (hrs)	Raingear	Boots	Tennis Shoes	Carry Water	Take Food	Swimming	Waterfalls	Views	Historical Sites	Fruits
1	Diamond Head	X				.7	1	550	4	¼			X	X	X			X	X	
2	Black Point	X				1	½		3	¼						X				
3	Old Pali Highway	X				.3	¼		7	¼				X				X	X	X
4	Judd Memorial	X				1.3L	1		6	¼			X	X		X				X
5	Makiki Valley								3	¼										
	Kanealole	X				.7	½	500					X	X	X			X		X
	Makiki Valley	X				1.1	1						X	X	X			X		X
	Makiki Branch A	X				.7	½	500					X	X	X			X		X
6	Tantalus								6	¼										
	Manoa Cliffs		X			3	2	500				X	X	X	X			X	X	X
	Puu Ohia		X			2	1½	500				X	X	X	X			X	X	X
7	Manoa Falls	X				.8	1	800	3	¼		X	X			X	X			X
8	Waahila Ridge		X			2	2	700	4	¼			X	X	X			X		X
9	Lanipo			X		3	3	1600	6	½	X			X	X			X		
10	Wiliwilinui			X		3	3	2000	10	½	X			X	X			X		
11	Hanauma Bay								12	½										
	Koko Head	X				1	½	450					X	X	X			X		
	Koko Crater			X		1	1	1000					X	X	X			X	X	
	Blowhole		X			2	1½						X	X	X	X		X		
12	Puu Piei			X		.8	1	1700	26	1	X			X				X		
13	Sacred Falls	X				2.2	1¼		28	1¼			X	X	X	X	X			X
14	Hauula								30	1¼										
	Hauula		X			2.5L	1¼	600					X	X	X			X		
	Maakua Gulch			X		3	3	1100			X	X	X	X		X	X			
	Papali		X			2.5L	2	800					X	X	X			X		
15	Laie			X		2	2	1400	36	1½	X			X	X	X	X	X		X
16	Aiea Loop		X			4.8L	3		12	½	X	X	X	X	X			X		X
17	Waimano				X	7.1	4	1600	14	½	X	X		X	X	X		X		
18	Manana				X	6	4	1700	15	½	X	X		X	X	X		X		
19	Wahiawa			X		4	3	650	22	1	X	X	X	X	X	X		X		
20	Poamoho Valley	X				3	2	1000	22	1	X	X	X	X	X	X	X			
21	Poamoho Ridge			X		3.4	3	800	28	1½	X	X		X	X			X		
22	Dupont				X	4	5	3800	30	1½	X	X		X	X			X		
23	Mokuleia			X		5.4	5	1900	32	1½	X	X		X	X			X		
24	Peacock Flats	X				3.5	3	1600	40	2½	X	X		X	X			X		
25	Kaneaki Heiau	X				.5	½		36	1½				X					X	X
26	Kaena Point	X				2	1½		42	2			X	X	X	X				

Camping

Hiking can be an exciting way to see Oahu, and camping can make your visit an inexpensive one. Since camping is a popular activity with local people, make your plans in advance and obtain permits as soon as you arrive on the island. There is one state campground on the island and 15 county beach parks where camping is permitted. The best part is that camping is free.

The only campground in the state park system on Oahu is at Keaiwa Heiau State Park. Reservations are required, and camping permits are granted for a maximum of one week. Reservations may be made by mail, but the applications must be received by the Department of State Parks at least seven calendar days in advance of the date the permit is to be in effect. (All addresses are in the appendix.) The campground is in a shaded, wooded area of the park, near the trailhead of the Aiea Loop Trail (Hiking Area No. 16).

The City of Honolulu operates 63 recreational areas located on all parts of the island. Camping is permitted at 15 places, all of which are beach parks. Permits are not issued earlier than two weeks before the day of occupancy. Camping is allowed for up to one week. Permits can be obtained from the Department of Parks and Recreation in Honolulu or at any of 10 satellite city halls located around the island. (All addresses are in the appendix.) All the campgrounds have cold-water showers, drinking water and restrooms. Most of the beach parks receive heavy use, so they are not always clean and the facilities are not always all in good operating order. The campgrounds at Waimanalo, Swanzy, Kahana Bay, Punaluu, Moku-leia, Keaau, Makaha, Lualualei, Nanakuli and Kahe are recommended, since they are usually clean and they have ample space for camping. Trailer camping is permitted at all of the parks where tents are allowed except Lualualei Beach Park and at Kaaawa Beach Park. Trailers must be self-contained, since there are no electrical or sewer connections.

The camper should keep in mind that most of the campsites on Oahu are in heavily populated areas or in areas accessible to population centers. Consequently, all of the ills—thievery, damage to equipment, drunkenness—of urban living are present. Campers should not leave valuables and equipment unattended or unprotected.

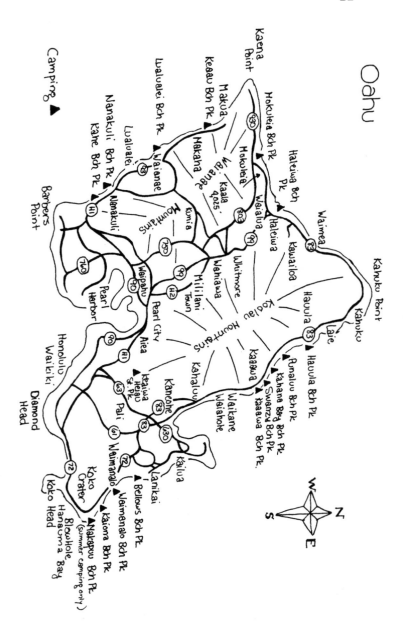

Food and Equipment

The following equipment is recommended for day hikes.

Knapsack
Hiking boots, strong shoes, or tennis shoes
Canteen, quart size (one per person)
Scout or Swiss Army knife
Insect repellent
Shorts
Bathing suit
Sunburn lotion and/or preventive
Sun glasses
Whistle for each child
Camera and film
Hiking Oahu—The Capital Isle
Hat
Optional:
    Poncho or raingear
    Towel
    Waterproof matches
    Flashlight

Planning and preparation are particularly important for the backpacker. The following equipment is recommended for overnight hikes and for campers.

BACKPACK CHECKLIST
  General Equipment:
    Frame and pack
    Lightweight sleeping bag or blanket
    Tube tent or nylon tent with rain fly—rain is common in
      most areas
    Plastic ground cover—the ground is damp in most areas
    Sleep pad
    Canteen, quart size
    Scout or Swiss Army knife
    Flashlight
    40 feet of nylon cord
    First-aid kit

Cooking Gear
Backpack stove
Fuel
Cooking pots
Sierra cup
Waterproof matches

Clothing
Poncho or raingear—A MUST
Pants
Shorts and/or bathing suit
Hat or bandana
Undershorts
T-shirts
Socks
Hiking boots

Toilet Articles
Soap (biodegradable)
Toothbrush/powder-paste
Part-roll toilet paper
Chapstick
Comb
Washcloth and towel
Insect repellent
Sunburn lotion or preventive

Miscellaneous
Sun glasses
Camera and film
Plastic bags
Fishing gear

Hawaiian Made Easy

For your interest, throughout the text wherever a Hawaiian place name is used, I have provided a literal translation if possible. In many instances, Hawaiian names have multiple meanings and even the experts sometimes disagree over the literal meaning. The meanings given here are based on the best information available and on the context in which the name is used. As students of the environment, the Hawaiians had a flair for finding the most expressive words to describe their physical surroundings.

Most visitors are reluctant to try to pronounce Hawaiian words. But with a little practice and a knowledge of some simple rules, you can develop some language skill and add to your Hawaiian experience. Linguists regard Hawaiian as one of the most fluid and melodious languages of the world. There are only 12 letters in the Hawaiian alphabet: five vowels, a,e,i,o,u, and seven consonants, h,k,l,m,n,p,w. Hawaiian is spelled phonetically. Correct pronunciation is easy if you do not try to force English pronunciation onto the Hawaiian language. Vowel sounds are simple: a=ah; e=eh; i=ee; o=oh; and u=oo. Consonant sounds are the same as in English with the exception of w. Rules for w are not adhered to with any consistency by local people. Generally, w is pronounced "w" at the beginning of a word and after a. For example, Waimea is pronounced "Wai-may-ah" and wala-wala is "Wah-lah-wah-lah." Hawaiians also usually pronounce w as "w" when it follows o or u: auwaha is "ah-oo-wah-hah," and hoowali is "hoh-oh-wah-lee." When w is next to the final letter of a word, it is variably pronounced "w" and "v"; Wahiawa is "wah-he-ah-wa," but Hawi is "ha-vee." Listen to the locals for their treatment of this sound. Since the Hawaiian language is not strongly accented, the visitor will probably be understood without employing any accent.

Part II:

Hiking Trails on Oahu

16

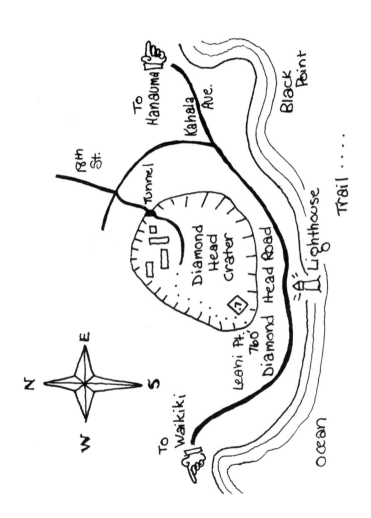

DIAMOND HEAD

(Hiking Area No. 1)

Rating: Family.

Features: Panorama of greater Honolulu area, historical site, extinct volcanic crater.

Permission: Division of State Parks, 1151 Punchbowl St., Room 310, Honolulu, Oahu, 96813 (Phone 548-7455).

Hiking Distance & Time: .7 miles, 1 hour, 550-foot gain.

Driving Instructions: From Honolulu (4 miles, ¼ hour) drive south on Kalakaua Ave., right on Diamond Head Road and around to east side of crater, left at sign marked "Civ-Alert USPFO" opposite 18th St. Follow road through tunnel into crater to parking area on left.

Bus Instructions: From Waikiki take the Beach bus to Kahala Ave./Diamond Head Road. Walk up Diamond Head Road to road marked "Civ-Alert USPFO" and follow the road into the crater.

Introductory Notes: Although the hike to the summit of Diamond Head is hot and dry, the panorama offered from the top and along the rim trail is striking. This is a "must" hike for the whole family. Although a large portion of the crater and the surrounding area are on a military reservation, the hiking trail is under the jurisdiction of the Division of State Parks.

Without question, Diamond Head is the most photographed and the most readily identifiable place in Hawaii. Before the arrival of Western man, the area was known as Leahi (lit., "casting point"). In the early 1800's British sailors found calcite crystals in the rocks on the slopes of the crater and thought they

were diamonds. Following the discovery, the tuff
crater was called Kaimana-Hila (lit., "Diamond Hill"),
and today the world-famous place is known as Diamond Head. Geologists estimate that the crater was
formed some 100,000 years ago by violent steam ex-
plosions. During World War II Diamond Head was an
important bastion for the protection of the island.
Gun emplacements, lookout towers, and tunnels were
concealed in and on the walls of the crater. Although
abandoned in recent years, these places are interesting
to investigate, particularly for children. It is helpful
to carry a flashlight, since the trail passes through two
short tunnels and up a spiral stairway.

On the Trail: The trailhead on the northwest side of
the parking area is marked, and the trail is easy to follow to the summit. Kiawe (*Prosopis pallida*) trees
abound on the floor of the crater. These valuable
trees with fernlike leaves and thorny branches are the
descendants of a single seed planted by Father Bache-
lot, a priest, in 1828 in his churchyard in Honolulu.
The tree is a source not only of fuel and lumber but
also of honey (produced from the flower), medicine,
tannin and fodder, which is produced from its bean-
like yellow pods containing 25% grape sugar.

As you continue along the gently rising trail to
the first concrete landing and lookout, you should be
able to identify a number of birds. Two species of
doves, the barred dove (*Geopelia striata*) and the
spotted dove (*Streptopelia chinensis*), are common
and abundant on Oahu. The spotted dove, the larger
of the two, has a band of black around the sides and
back of the neck which is spotted with white. The
barred dove is pale brown above, gray below, and
barred with black. You should also see the beautiful,
bright red, male cardinal (*Richmondena cardinalis*)
with its orange beak and black face.

The concrete landing is the first of many lookout points along the trail. You have a good view of the crater and are able to distinguish some of the bunkers and gun emplacements on the slopes and on the crest of the crater. Follow the steps and the pipe railing to the first tunnel. You cannot see daylight at the end of the tunnel, because it turns to the left at midpoint. A flashlight is not necessary to pass through the tunnel safely, but it is a comfort to small children since it *is* dark. As you leave the tunnel, investigate the rooms in the concrete building opposite the exit, which were used for supplies and contained a power unit. Look for the bunker behind the building and hike to the left to a viewpoint overlooking the crater. A steep staircase—99 steps—leads the hiker into a short tunnel at the end of which is an observation room and the first view of Waikiki and the greater Honolulu area. Look for the room containing a spiral stairway. Climb

Waikiki from inside bunker atop Leahi Point

the stairway and then the ladder which takes you to the top and to the summit of Diamond Head. The concrete building at the summit is situated on top of Leahi Point at an elevation of 760 feet. Keep a watchful eye on children, for the summit's flanks are precipitous. The observation point at the summit provides a shady and comfortable picnic spot as well as a panoramic view.

It is possible to hike completely around the rim of the crater and to return to the parking lot by cutting through the brush, but the trail is steep and dangerous due to loose volcanic rock and ash. Only confident hikers should attempt this alternative route to the parking area. You will find numerous observation points and gun emplacements around the rim similar to those at the summit.

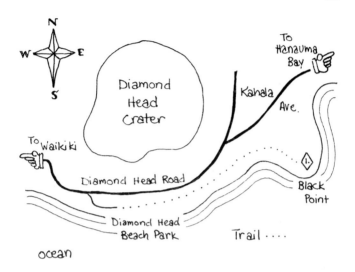

BLACK POINT

(Hiking Area No. 2)

Rating: Family.

Features: Beach hike, tidepools, swimming, good surfing.

Permission: None.

Hiking Distance & Time: 1 mile, ½ hour.

Driving Instructions: From Honolulu (3 miles, ¼ hour) drive south on Kalakaua Ave., then right on Diamond Head Road to Diamond Head Beach Park or to a parking turnout off the road overlooking the beach.

Bus Instructions: From Waikiki take the Beach bus to Diamond Head Beach Park. Walk to the beach and trailhead.

Introductory Notes: Hiking the shoreline anywhere in Hawaii is a delight for the whole family. Swimming and surfing are good at Diamond Head Beach, so there are a lot of wahines ("girls") and kanes ("boys") on the beach. There are also other interesting beach sights, such as tidepools.

On the Trail: Begin the hike anywhere along Diamond Head Beach Park and walk east. The Diamond Head Lighthouse to the west marks the finish line for the annual Trans-Pac Yacht Race. The surf is rated good by locals, and the beach is less crowded than Waikiki. The cliffs bordering the beach provide a barrier from the noise and the crowds of Honolulu. Haalawai (lit., "the water basalt") Beach at the midpoint of the hike is rated as a safe swimming beach. It is a good place to relax, to picnic, and to watch the surfers and other beach sights. Hike out to Kupikipikio (lit., "rough") Point, or Black Point, as it is more commonly called, for tidepools and for some interesting lava formations shaped by the crashing sea. Black Point is a place where you can spend a few relaxing hours or a full day only a short distance from one of the most crowded beaches in the world.

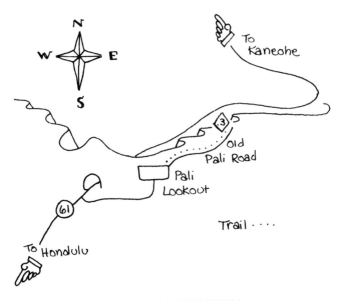

OLD PALI HIGHWAY

(Hiking Area No. 3)

Rating: Family.

Features: Superb views of east side, historical site.

Permission: None.

Hiking Distance & Time: .3 miles, ¼ hour.

Driving Instructions: From Honolulu (7 miles, ¼ hour) drive northwest on H-1, then right on Route 61 (Pali Highway) and follow signs to Pali Lookout.

Bus Instructions: No bus service to Nuuanu Pali Lookout.

Introductory Notes: While Diamond Head is probably the most photographed place on Oahu, the Nuuanu Pali (lit., "cool height cliff") is probably the most visited. The Nuuanu Pali offers a stunning view of the east side; it is a place of historical importance, and it is a spot where very strong winds return objects thrown by visitors. From the lookout and along

the short trail, the broad panorama of the east side
spans from Lanikai in the southeast to Kailua and
Kaneohe below the Pali to Kahaluu in the north. The
distinctive Mokapu (lit., "taboo district") Peninsula
to the northeast is the place, according to Hawaiian
legend, where man was created. Some believe that the
four great gods, Kane, Kanaloa, Ku and Lono, met
here. Kane and Kanaloa made images of themselves
in the dirt and then argued over which one had the
power to create man. While Kanaloa's image turned
to stone, Kane's image came to life and became a
man after Kane said "Come alive," and Ku and Lono
responded, "Live." Kane's man was named Wakea,
and some believe he was the ancestor of all Hawaiians. As Wakea walked, he noticed that his shadow
always followed him. When he awoke the next mor-
ning, he found a beautiful woman lying by his side.
He thought that the gods had changed his shadow
into a woman, so he called her Keakuahulilani, "the
shadow made of heaven."

Nuuanu Pali is the site of a significant and tragic
battle that took place in 1795, the year in which
Kamehameha the Great added Oahu to his kingdom.
His forces drove the Oahu warriors up to the Pali and
overwhelmed them. One account records that 300
warriors were driven over the cliff by Kamehameha's
forces. Another story says that the defeated army
jumped to its death rather than surrender.

On the Trail: This short trail begins on an 1,186-foot-
high perch in the Kaneohe Forest Reserve known as
the Nuuanu Pali Lookout. At the Pali, there is a break
in the Koolau (lit., "windward") Mountain Range that
has given Honolulu travelers a route to the east side
for hundreds of years. Originally a footpath, it was
made a horse trail in 1845 and later widened to
accommodate carriages. Today a modern highway
and a tunnel through the mountain speed travelers

over the pali. A ramp to the right of the lookout leads
to the old Pali Road. Gale-force winds prevent easy
passage to the road, so hold on to all that you value!
There is no wind on the old road, so pause frequently
to enjoy and to photograph the fluted palisades and
the richly foliated 3000-foot peaks of the Koolau
Range. It is a breath-taking sight, for the mountains
drop abruptly to the valley, and the pasture land below stretches to the sea.

Proceed down the road with some caution, since
the road is wet and slippery in places, and falling
rocks and boulders present a hazard. Look for a small
stream on the right a few hundred yards from the
lookout. Walk up the stream a short distance to a
small waterfall and a delightful place to picnic.

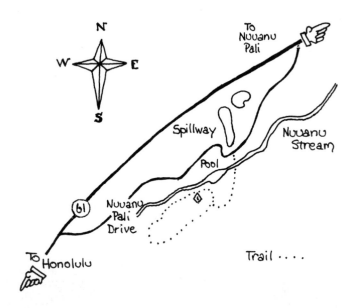

JUDD MEMORIAL

(Hiking Area No. 4)

Rating: Family.

Features: Swimming, mud-sliding, introduced flora.

Permission: None.

Hiking Distance & Time: 1.3 mile loop, 1 hour.

Driving Instructions: From Honolulu (6 miles, ¼ hour) drive northwest on H-1, right on Route 61 (Pali Highway), right on Nuuanu Pali Drive, and .7 mile past Kimo Drive to Reservoir No. 2 spillway.

Bus Instructions: From Waikiki take the Nuuanu-Punahou bus to Nuuanu Pali Drive/Kimo Drive. Walk up Nuuanu Pali Drive to the trailhead.

Introductory Notes: The hike to the Jackass-ginger pool in Nuuanu Stream is an easy and delightful outing for the family—even though mosquitoes are plentiful. Be certain to take old clothes, lunch, insect repellent, and a piece of plastic for mud-sliding.

On the Trail: The trail begins east of the spillway and downhill from the road and reaches Nuuanu (lit., "cool height") Stream after a few hundred feet. Large stream rocks make a convenient bridge to cross the stream, but do so with caution. Across the stream the trail enters a bamboo thicket, climbs into a eucalyptus grove, and continues into a stand of Norfolk Island pines (*Araucaria excelsa*). Native to Norfolk Island near Australia, these perfectly symmetrical evergreens were introduced to the Islands to be used as windbreaks and for timber. The smaller trees are used locally as Christmas trees. Designated as

Jackass ginger pool

the Charles S. Judd Memorial Grove in 1953, this forest of planted trees was so named in honor of the first Territorial Forester. There are numerous mud-sliding chutes in the area where it is possible, when they are wet, to toboggan down the hill on a plastic sheet, on pili grass or on ti leaves. The latter was the traditional Hawaiian conveyance. Mud-sliding is an ancient Hawaiian sport particularly popular with Hawaiian royalty. Look for a wet place and give it a try. The nearby stream is a convenient place to wash off the mud.

The trail follows the forest-reserve boundary near a residential area and then turns downhill toward Nuuanu Stream through a maze of guava and hau brush. A short distance from this dense thicket, the trail passes above the Jackass-ginger pool. From here, a number of spur trails and mud-sliding chutes lead to the pool below. Don't miss the pool and a chance to swim and picnic.

To return to the trailhead, retrace your steps up the hillside to the point from which you descended and continue southeast and then north (left) along the initial portion of the trail which will return you to the road. A shorter route to the trailhead goes north from the pool through the bushes a short distance to the Nuuanu Pali Drive. Once on the road, walk east (right) to the trailhead.

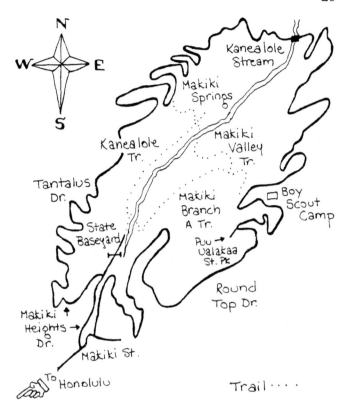

MAKIKI VALLEY

(Hiking Area No. 5)

Rating: Family.

Features: Fruits, Job's Tears, native and introduced flora.

Permission: None.

Hiking Distance & Time: See individual hikes.

Driving Instructions: From Honolulu (3 miles, ¼ hour) drive up Makiki St., turn left on Makiki Heights Dr. and continue straight on paved drive into Forestry "baseyard" (2135 Makiki Heights

Dr.). Park off road outside the chain gate even if it
is not locked.

Bus Instructions: From Waikiki take the Waikiki-
Liliha bus to Beretania Street/Kalakaua Ave. Go
under the freeway and walk up Makiki Street and
left on Makiki Heights Drive to the trailhead.

Introductory Notes: There are three trails in Makiki
(the valley was named after a type of stone found
here that was used as a weight for an octupus lure)
Valley. To cover the three trails and to make a convenient loop hike, begin your hike at the Kanealole
Trailhead in the Division of Forestry baseyard, since
it is the easiest trailhead to locate. I recommend
that you go up the Kanealole Trail, hike east on the
Makiki Valley Trail, and return south on the Makiki
Branch A Trail, completing a 2-mile loop from the
baseyard.

**On the Trail: Kanealole Trail, .7 mile, ½ hour, 500-
foot gain (trail rating: family)** (The trail is signed
Makiki Valley Trail at the baseyard.)

The trail on the west side of Kanealole Stream is
usually wet and muddy, but it is a gentler ascent than
the Makiki Branch A Trail on the east side. Our trail
follows an old road which is used by work crews who
control the growth in the valley. Although the hike is
uphill, there is abundant shade along the trail, which
makes for a fairly cool and enjoyable hike for the
whole family.

**Makiki Valley Trail, 1.1 miles, 1 hour (trail rating:
family)**

This trail traverses Makiki Valley in a west-east
direction. The trailhead on the west side is about 2
miles up Tantalus Drive from Makiki Heights Drive,
north of a eucalyptus grove where the road makes a
sharp turn. The trailhead on the east side is on the
left side of the road just past the Boy Scout camp on
Round Top Road. This trailhead is .7 mile north of

the entrance of Puu Ualakaa (lit., "rolling sweet-potato hill") State Park.

From the Tantalus Drive trailhead, the trail descends eastward through a forest into Makiki Valley until it meets the Kanealole Trail. At this junction, pause and find the springs in the brush to the left of the junction. The grass and brush should be matted where other hikers have made their way to the springs, 30 feet north of the junction. It is an enchanting place to pause to enjoy the beauty and the solitude. It is also a place to pick Job's tears (*Coix lacryma-jobi*), which are abundant. The black, blue-gray and white, pea-sized beans of this plant are favorites with local people, who string them into attractive necklaces, leis and rosaries. Ranging from one to six feet high, the plant is a coarse, branched grass with long, pointed leaves. The beans are easy for

Jobs tears at Makiki Springs

children to string with a needle and heavy thread.

From the junction, the trail turns in and out of small gulches and crosses a couple of small streams, passing through a richly foliated, forested valley. One of the many delights along this trail is the mountain apple (*Eugenia malaccensis*), which is abundant and within easy reach. Indeed, there is no other place in Hawaii where I have seen these succulent red apples growing in such profusion. What a treat! From the junction with the Makiki Branch A Trail, the valley trail ascends the ridge to the trailhead on Round Top Drive.

Makiki Branch A Trail, .7 miles, ½ hour, 555-foot gain or loss (trail rating: family). (The trail is signed *Makiki Ridge Trail* at the baseyard.)

From the junction with the Makiki Valley Trail, the hike on the Makiki Branch A trail is an easy downhill walk. The trail contours along Makiki Ridge, passing through juniper, eucalyptus, and bamboo in the lower portion. Periodically, a break in the forest provides a good view of Honolulu and of Manoa Valley to the east. One of the most interesting trees in the valley is the octopus, or umbrella, tree (*Brassaia actinophylla*), whose peculiar blossoms look like the long, spreading arms of an octopus. The new blossoms are first greenish-yellow, then light pink, and finally deep red. As the trail levels, it crosses a foot bridge over the stream, passes through the territorial nursery, and returns to the baseyard.

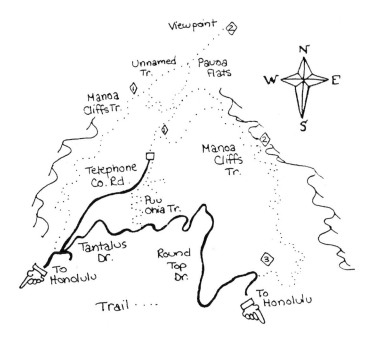

TANTALUS

(Hiking Area No. 6)

Rating: Hardy family.

Features: Valley views, fruits, native and introduced flora.

Permission: None.

Hiking Distance & Time: See individual hikes.

Driving Instructions: From Honolulu (6 miles, ¼ hour) drive up Makiki Street, turn left on Makiki Heights Dr., then go right on Tantalus Drive three miles to the top, where there are a telephone-service road on the left and a trailhead marker.

Bus Instructions: No bus service on Tantalus Drive or Round Top Drive.

Introductory Notes: Tantalus and Round Top drives combine to make a popular auto tour above Honolulu. The many turnouts, which provide panoramas of Honolulu, are favorites of visitors and locals in the daytime and lovers in the evening. The two hikes that lead into the mountains from the top of the road are a delight for the whole family. Local students gave the name "Tantalus" to this area after the mythical Greek king. Tantalus Mountain (2013 feet) was so named, it is suggested, because as the students hiked, the peak seemed to recede. (You may recall that Tantalus was punished by being made to stand in a pool of water which receded each time he tried to drink.)

You have the choice of three trailheads for the hikes included in this area (see the map). I suggest that you begin your hiking either at the Manoa Cliffs trailhead on Tantalus Drive or at the Puu Ohia trailhead, where Tantalus Drive becomes Round Top Drive. The Manoa Cliffs trailhead on Round Top Drive is more difficult to find and to park at.

On the Trail: Manoa Cliffs, 3 miles, 2 hours, 500-foot gain (trail rating: hardy family)

Just 3 miles up Tantalus Drive, a sign identifying the trail and a spur road which leads to a Hawaiian Telephone Co. facility mark the trailhead for the Manoa (lit., "vast") Cliffs Trail. The trail is well-maintained and easy to follow. You are likely to share the trail with students from the University of Hawaii, since the area is used as an outdoor classroom. The initial, forested portion (1.2 miles) contours the hillside. A number of native and introduced plants, some of which are identified by markers, are found along the trail. According to the Division of Forestry, 33 native species of flora have been identified. You should not have any trouble finding two introduced plants whose fruit is edible. Guava (*Psid-*

On the Manoa Cliffs Trail

ium guajava) trees are particularly abundant throughout the area. The yellow, lemon-sized fruit is a tasty
treat high in Vitamin C. Red thimbleberries (*Rubus
rosaefolius*), which are also profuse, grow on a small,
thorny bush with white flowers.

About 1 mile from the trailhead, you reach a junction. The trail to the left (north) is well-defined and
will eventually join the Puu Ohia Trail at Pauoa Flats.
You may choose to continue on this unnamed trail
and to return to the Manoa Cliffs Trail via the Puu
Ohia Trail. At the junction with the unnamed trail,
the Manoa Cliffs Trail makes a sharp right and follows
switchbacks up a hill for 0.2 mile to the Manoa Cliffs/
Puu Ohia trails junction (actually, a pair of junctions
30 feet apart). Puu Ohia leads north (left) down the
hill and south (right) up the hill while the cliffs trail
continues east.

The remaining part of the Manoa Cliffs Trail hike
contours the hillside above Manoa Valley. Spectacular
views of the valley are possible from a number of
viewpoints. Keep a sharp eye on small children, however, for parts of the hillside along the trail are steep.
There are a number of overgrown trails used by pig
hunters leading off both sides of the trail which
should be avoided. One spur trail, a short distance
east from the Manoa Cliffs/Puu Ohia junction, switchbacks up the hill to meet the Puu Ohia Trail. The
Manoa Cliffs Trail turns south and emerges on Round
Top Drive at the other trailhead for this hike.

It is 1.4 miles west (right) to your car via the road
or 0.9 mile west to the Puu Ohia trailhead.

**Puu Ohia Trail, 2 miles, 1½ hours, 500-foot gain (trail
rating: hardy family)**

The Puu Ohia (lit., "ohia tree hill") Trailhead is
easy to find. It is .5 miles from the Manoa Cliffs
Trailhead near the uppermost point of Round Top
and Tantalus drives, where you will find a large park-

Bamboo forest on the Puu Ohia Trail

ing area opposite the trailhead (the nearest street number is 4050). The first .5 miles of the trail follows a circuitous route up a hill. The trail then straightens and goes along the side of the ridge a short distance to where a number of trails lead off down to the right. These trails lead to a popular pig-hunting area, and should be avoided. Bear left and follow the trail

to where it meets a paved road, then follow the road
to its end at a Hawaiian Telephone Co. facility. The
trail continues north from behind and to the left of
the telephone building and descends to join the
Manoa Cliffs Trail. As you descend, bear to the left
to avoid the somewhat overgrown pig trails to the
right and the one clear spur trail also on the right.
This latter trail eventually meets the Manoa Cliffs
Trail farther east. Soon you cross this trail, jogging
right 10 yards on it. The Puu Ohia Trail is wide but
steep, so proceed with caution until you reach Pauoa
Flats. Although the trail over the flats is level, it is
usually wet and slippery and it has exposed roots
which are potential ankle-busters.

Eucalyptus (*Eucalyptus robusta*) and paper-bark
(*Melaleuca leucadendra*) trees dominate the flats area.
The eucalyptus has thick, pointed leaves with a cap-
sule type of fruit, while the distinguishing feature of
the paper-bark tree is bark that can be peeled in
sheets. This tree has been planted on the islands for
conservation purposes in wet, boggy areas. There are
a number of secondary trails on the flats where hikers
have cut through the bamboo to vistas overlooking
Manoa Valley to the east (right). Continue north
(straight ahead) on the main trail to a lookout for a
fantastic view of Nuuanu Valley, the Pali Highway,
and Reservoir No. 4 in the Honolulu Watershed Forest Reserve. DO NOT hike beyond the lookout into
the watershed area, which is protected by both law
and good judgment.

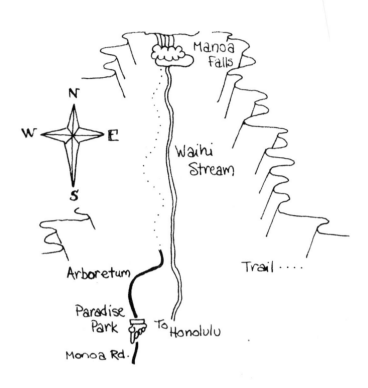

MANOA FALLS

(Hiking Area No. 7)

Rating: Family.

Features: Waterfall, swimming, fruits.

Permission: None.

Hiking Distance & Time: .8 mile, 1 hour, 800-foot gain.

Driving Instructions: From Honolulu (3 miles, ¼ hour) drive north on Manoa Road past Paradise Park and Lyon Arboretum to the end of the road.

Bus Instructions: From Waikiki or Ala Moana Center take the Manoa-Waikiki bus to Paradise Park at the end of the line. Walk up the road to the trailhead.

Introductory Notes: The trail to Manoa (lit., "vast") Falls is easily accessible from downtown Honolulu, which probably accounts for its popularity. You can expect to share the trail and the pool with local people as well as visitors. Nevertheless, pack a lunch and make the trip to the falls, for it is worth the time. To reduce the risk of a break-in, park your car in the lot at Paradise Park and walk the short distance to the end of the road.

On the Trail: A chain gate and a foot bridge at the end of the road mark the trailhead for the hike into Manoa Valley along Waihi (lit., "trickling water") Stream. Most of the trail is muddy and a bit slippery because heavy rains have washed away soil around trees and exposed their roots. The heavy rains also sustain a heavily foliated area where vegetation common to damp areas is abundant. The trail is easy to follow through the forest reserve. There are some fruit trees along the trail, but the likelihood of finding fruit is slim because of the popularity of the hike. The yellow, lemon-sized guava may be found as well as the popular mountain apple. This succulent apple is small and red, has a thin, waxy skin, and is usually ripe in June.

At midpoint, the canyon narrows and the footing becomes wetter. There are a number of larger pools where you may see hikers swimming or catching prawns, crayfish or frogs. The latter are particularly plentiful. You should be able to see the falls from a number of points along the trail. The junglelike setting at the falls makes for an enchanting place to swim and picnic if it is not too crowded.

The Division of Forestry prohibits entry into the closed watershed beyond the falls. Violators might damage a protected area and face the prospect of court appearances and fines. Furthermore, numerous injuries and a few fatalities have been recorded as a result of people hiking in this prohibited area.

Manoa Falls

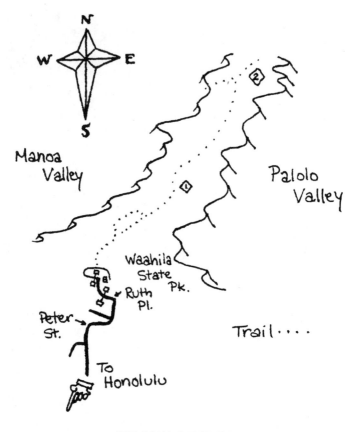

WAAHILA RIDGE

(Hiking Area No. 8)

Rating: Hardy family.

Features: Views of Honolulu and Manoa Valley, fruits, native and introduced flora.

Permission: None.

Hiking Distance & Time: 2 miles, 2 hours, 700-foot gain.

Driving Instructions: From Honolulu (4 miles, ¼ hour) drive north up St. Louis Drive, turn left on

Peter St., and then left on Ruth Place to the entrance to Waahila State Park. Drive to the upper
end of the park.

Bus Instructions: From Waikiki take the St. Louis-
Kahala-Maunalani bus to the end of the line at
Peter Street/Ruth Place. Walk up Ruth Place to
Waahila Ridge State Park and to the trailhead.

Introductory Notes: Waahila Ridge State Park is a
good place close to Honolulu to picnic, to enjoy
a cool, forested park, and to share a hike with the
family.

On the Trail: Proceed northeast from the parking
area on a dirt road which is used to service the power-
transmission lines on the ridge. A number of paths
lead off the road into the guava trees, which are
plentiful, but the yellow, lemon-sized fruit may be
difficult to find because park visitors pick it as fast
as it ripens. At 0.4 mile, a trail goes left and then
shortly rejoins the road, which has by now narrowed
to a trail. The two trails meet under a cluster of poles
on top of the ridge. From under this network of
transmission lines, the trail follows the narrow
Waahila (the name of a female chief who excelled in a
dance named for her) Ridge, which separates Manoa
and Palolo (lit., "clay") valleys. The Norfolk Island
pines and other exotics bordering the trail were planted about 40 years ago in an effort to improve the
watershed and the esthetic and recreational value of
the ridge area. The trail makes a few steep descents
and ascents along the ridge, which require some caution, particularly if wet and muddy. The frequent
views of Manoa Valley and Honolulu through the
dense forest are striking. The majestic koa *(Acacia
koa)* tree can be seen in the valley and on the ridge. A
native of Hawaii, and frequently called Hawaiian
mahogany, the koa had a wide range of uses by
Hawaiians. It was prized for making canoes, and was

also used to make surfboards, calabashes, ukuleles, and a variety of household furniture. Growing to heights of 100 feet, the koa has a large trunk and crescent-shaped leaves.

At a junction at the 2-mile point you must turn around unless you wish to take the steeply descending trail on the left, which emerges on Alani Drive in Manoa Valley. To reach downtown Honolulu from the end of this trail, continue south on Alani Drive, right on East Manoa Road, and left on Oahu Ave., which becomes University Ave. just before reaching the campus of the University of Hawaii. You may choose to follow this trail if you do not have to return to the park for your vehicle.

Hiking from the junction on the trail to the summit of the Koolau Mountains is prohibited by law, since the ridge continues into the Honolulu Watershed Forest Reserve. There are other trails to the summit of the Koolau Range described in this book (Lanipo—Hiking Area No. 9—for example) which are legal to hike. The view from Lanipo is equal to that at the end of Waahila Ridge.

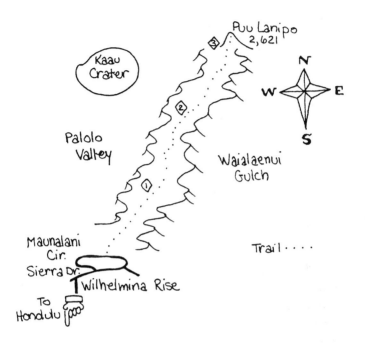

LANIPO

(Hiking Area No. 9)

Rating: Strenuous.

Features: View from Koolau Mountain Range, native and introduced flora.

Permission: None.

Hiking Distance & Time: 3 miles, 3 hours, 1,600-foot gain.

Driving Instructions: From Honolulu (6 miles, ½ hour) drive southeast on H-1 to Koko Head turn-off. Go left over freeway toward mountains, then right on Waialae Ave., and then take the first left, Wilhelmina Rise, to the top of the hill and Maunalani Circle, where a public-access passageway between fences marks the trailhead.

Bus Instructions: From Waikiki take the St. Louis Kahala-Maunalani bus to Sierra Drive/Lurline Drive. Walk up Sierra Drive to Maunalani Circle and to the trailhead.

Introductory Notes: The Lanipo and Wiliwilinui (Hiking Area No. 10) trails are parallel hikes to peaks along the Koolau Mountain Range. Indeed, an experienced and daring hiker could join the trails by hiking ½ mile along an extremely precipitous and dangerous ridge on the Koolau Range. Do not attempt this connecting hike alone. In any event, both hikes, while strenuous, are worth the effort, for the views from the summit of the east side of the island are stunning. Of the two, I prefer Lanipo because it is a 3-mile foot trail whereas the first 2½ miles of Wiliwilinui are on a jeep road. The Lanipo trail also skirts Kaau Crater.

On the Trail: The trail initially ascends along a fenced walkway for about 100 yards, to a point on Mauumae (lit., "wilted grass") Ridge. After a short descent, the trail traverses a number of saddles along the ridge. The first two saddles are a bit steep, with loose rock underfoot, so that caution is advised to avoid sore feet or a twisted ankle. The flora along the ridge is mostly low scrub and low trees, so that views of the surrounding area are unobstructed. To the west (left) Palolo (lit., "clay") Valley extends north to Kaau (lit., "forty") Crater which lies at the base of the Koolau Range ridge. The ¼-mile-wide crater, legend holds, was formed by the demigod Maui who, wanting to join Kauai and Oahu, threw out a great hook hoping to catch the foundation of Kauai. He gave a tremendous tug and loosed a rock. The rock fell at his feet where he was standing at Kaena Point on Oahu, while his hook sailed over his head and landed in Palolo Valley, creating Kaau Crater.

After the midpoint of the hike, the ridge narrows considerably. Thereafter, the trail is wet, muddy and steep, and it is necessary to grasp branches and roots of plants to continue. However, there are level places to rest and to enjoy a panorama of Diamond Head and the Honolulu area.

A variety of native plants can be identified. Look for the following: ulei (*Osteomeles anthyllidifolia*), a single, sweet-scented, thornless Hawaiian rose; kawau (*Byronia sandwicensis*) a Hawaiian holly tree with white blossoms and black berries; and the common yet beautiful and interesting ohia lehua (*Metrosideros collina*), a plant that varies in size from a shrub to a tree 100 feet tall. The leaves are usually small, rounded or blunt, and grayish, and the flower appears as a tuft of red stamens emerging from close-growing petals. Visitors frequently identify it as a bottlebrush tree due to the close similarity of the two. Both the lehua and the bottlebrush are in the myrtle family. Legend says that the lehua is a favorite of Pele, goddess of volcanoes, who will cause rain unless an offering is made before a lehua flower is picked.

The last ½ mile is steep and requires agility to climb the precipitous ridge, to make your way around thick brush, and to avoid mud holes. But the views from the summit are ample reward for your efforts. You have a sweeping view of the east side, from the town of Waimanalo (lit., "potable water") to the northeast, to Kailua (lit., "two seas") to the north, and along the magnificent Koolau Range extending west. All this, and a plentiful supply of thimble-berries, await the hiker at the summit. Puu Lanipo (lit., "dense peak") (2621 feet elevation) is to the east (right), on the way to the Wiliwilinui Trail.

WILIWILINUI

(Hiking Area No. 10)

Rating: Strenuous.

Features: Views from the Koolau Mountain Range, native flora and fauna.

Permission: None.

Hiking Distance & Time: 3 miles, 3 hours, 2000-foot gain.

Driving Instructions: From Honolulu (10 miles, ½ hour) drive southeast on H-1, which becomes Route 72. Turn left on Laukahi Street (0.6 mile from the end of the freeway and go 2 miles to the top of the road, where a gate bars driving access a city water-storage facility.

Bus Instruction: From Waikiki take the Beach bus to the stop opposite Laukahi Street near Waialae Country Club. Walk up Laukahi Street to the trailhead.

Introductory Notes: The Wiliwilinui and Lanipo (see Introductory Notes to Hiking Area No. 9) trails are parallel hikes to peaks along the Koolau Mountain Range. Both are viewful and worthwhile hikes.

On the Trail: The "No Trespassing" sign on the gate across the eroded asphalt road was placed there to prohibit driving access to the waterworks. It is legal to climb over or walk around the gate if locked, and to follow the road and then the foot trail to the summit. Four spur roads lead off the road in the first mile of the hike. At each junction, bear left and continue on the road along the ridge, which narrows considerably after the first mile. The road extends 2½ miles along the Wiliwilinui (lit., "large wiliwili"— a native tree bearing red seeds) Ridge overlooking Kapakahi (lit., "crooked") Gulch to the west and Wailupe (lit., "kite water") Gulch to the east. You should see numerous birds along the trail. The elepaio (*Chasiempis sanwichensis*), an endemic bird that is common throughout the forest, has a gray back, a rather long, blackish tail and a white rump. It is a somewhat noisy and curious bird, giving forth with what is best described as a sort of "wolf whistle." Another native bird, the apapane (*Himatione sanguinea*), can be found feeding on the nectar of the ohia flowers. It is a deep-crimson bird with black wings and tail and a slightly curved black bill.

In spite of the 2000-foot elevation gain to the summit, the route along the road is a relatively gentle ascent, but it can be muddy and wet by the time you reach the foot trail. lantana (*Lantana camara*) is a common flower that blossoms almost continuously in the surrounding forest. Its flowers vary in color from yellow to orange to pink to red. Another common yet delicate and pretty flower is the wild, or Philippine, orchid (*Spathoglottis plicata*). Usually lavender, it has what appear to be five starlike petals but are actually two petals and three sepals.

The road ends at about 1800 feet elevation and the foot trail extends to the summit, ½ mile and an 800-foot elevation gain distant. The climb on the foot trail is usually wet and muddy and somewhat treacherous. The view of the east side is magnificent, from Waimanalo to the east to Kualoa (lit., "long back") Point to the north-northwest. The trail to Lanipo goes west along the pali, if you dare to take it.

Hanauma Bay from Koko Crater

HANAUMA BAY

(Hiking Area No. 11)

Rating: See individual hikes.

Features: Swimming, snorkeling, tidepools, historical sites, blowhole, views of coastal area.

Permission: None.

Hiking Distance & Time: See individual hikes.

Driving Instructions: From Honolulu (12 miles, ½ hour) drive southeast on H-1, which becomes Route 72, then right on Hanauma Bay Road to parking lot.

Bus Instructions: From Waikiki take the Beach bus to Hanauma Bay turnoff. Consult map and text for trailheads.

Introductory Notes: To visit Oahu but fail to hike and swim at Hanauma is a mistake. Hanamua Bay is not only a strikingly beautiful place, but it also offers a variety of hiking experiences.

On the Trail: Koko Head Trail, 1 mile, ½ hour, 450-foot gain (trail rating: family)

For the protection of your vehicle and for convenience, park in the parking lot at the end of the bay road overlooking Hanauma Bay. To reach the trailhead, walk up the bay road to the highway (Route 72). A gate across a paved road on the left (west) prevents vehicular travel to the summit of Koko (lit., "blood") Head. Climb through the gate or walk around it for the short hike to the summit. Enchanting views of Hanauma (lit., "curved bay" or "hand-wrestling bay") Bay and a panorama of the surrounding area are had along the road. Koko Head is a 642-foot-high tuff cone and, according to legend, is the last place on Oahu that Pele, the goddess of vol-

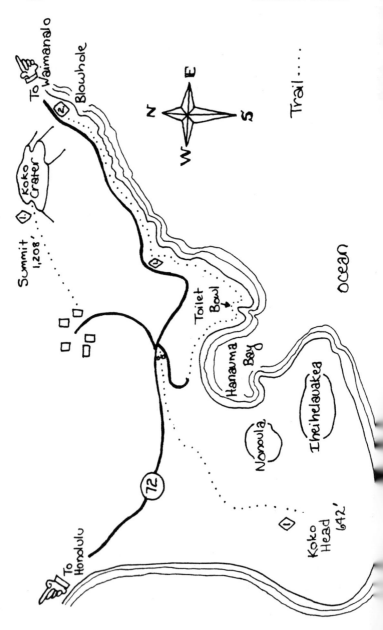

canoes, attempted to make a home for herself. From the summit, there are good views west to Diamond Head, north to the Koolau Mountain Range and Hawaii Kai (Henry Kaiser's 6000-acre town development) and northeast to Koko Crater and the coastline around Hanauma. Two small craters are below the summit to the east: Nonoula (lit., "red sunburned") on the left and Iheihelauakea (lit., "wide-leafed ihiihi"—an extinct or unknown plant that may have grown here) on the right. Look directly east and, if it is clear, you should see the island of Molokai some 20 miles across the channel. If you decide to return to the bay by crossing the two craters below, proceed with caution. There is no trail, and the slopes on the bay side of the craters are precipitous and dangerous.

Koko Crater, 1 mile, 1 hour, 1000-foot gain (trail rating: strenuous)

To reach the trailhead from Hanauma Bay, return to the main highway (Route 72). Take the road opposite the bay road by the sign identifying the "Aloha Hawaii Job Corps Training Center." It is ½ mile to the main office, behind which you will find an abandoned inclined railroad which leads directly to the summit.

The railroad ties make a convenient stepped path. Portions of the track are overgrown, so you can expect to have your arms and legs scratched by the brush. Be cautious when you cross over a gulch on a trestle about halfway to the summit. You should also be cautious when walking on the steps and platforms of the abandoned station on the summit, because the wood is broken and rotted in many places. The views from the old powerhouse and the 1208-foot lookout offer a 360° panorama. The Koolau Mountain Range to the north, Diamond Head and Hawaii Kai to the west, Koko Head and Hanauma Bay to the south, and the shoreline to the east treat the eye and calm the spirit after a hard climb. The crater, 1000 feet below, contains a botanical garden and bridle trails. Kohe-lepelepe (lit., "fringed vagina") was the old name for the crater.

Hanauma Bay to Blowhole, 2 miles, 1½ hours (trail rating: hardy family)

In 1967 Hanauma Bay was declared a marine-life conservation district, which meant that no marine life could be caught here or injured in any manner. Consequently, it is a delightful experience to investigate tidepools or to snorkel and to observe the variety of sea life underwater. Hanauma Bay was once a crater, until the sea broke through the southeast crater wall.

From the beach, hike along the shelf above the water on the east side of the bay. Be alert not only for interesting tidepools but also for waves which may splash onto the shelf. While the danger of being overcome by a wave is slight, it is wise to keep a watchful eye on the water. Be certain to visit the popular "toilet bowl" just beyond the far end of the bay. This interesting feature is a hole about 30 feet in circumference and 10 feet deep which is alternately filled and emptied from beneath as waves come in and recede. Bathers jump or slide into the bowl as it fills. Then, to escape, they scramble out when the water rises to the top of the bowl. Try it. It's different!

From the "toilet bowl" you can climb to the ridge overlooking the bay or follow the coastline around Palea (lit., "brushed aside") Point. From here to the blowhole you are likely find many local people fishing and snorkeling, so pause to examine their catches and to exchange pleasantries. You will find that a smile and an inquisitive attitude will usually make a friend.

After the first mile, you may choose to hike to the road and to follow it to the blowhole, since the ledge above the water is narrow, and one needs some agility

full
toilet
bowl

to climb, crawl and jump over the lava while trying to avoid the crashing surf. However, by timing the waves and by using good judgment, you can make it to the blowhole at Halona (lit., "peering place") Point. A blowhole is a narrow vent in the lava through which water is forced by the charging surf. The blowhole at Halona Point "blows" water geysers 30-50 feet into the air, depending on surf conditions. It is a happy terminus to a delightful hike.

mpty
toilet
bowl

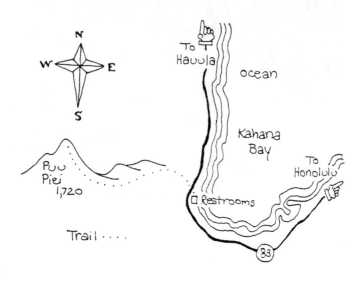

PUU PIEI

(Hiking Area No. 12)

Rating: Strenuous.

Features: Views of Kahana Bay and the nearby coastline.

Permission: None.

Hiking Distance & Time: .8 mile, 1 hour, 1700-foot gain.

Driving Instructions: From Honolulu (26 miles, 1 hour) drive northwest on H-1, then right on Route 61 (Pali Highway), then left on Route 83 to Kahana Bay Beach Park. Park north of the restrooms.

Bus Instructions: From Ala Moana Center take the Honolulu-Kaneohe-Wahiawa bus to Kahana Beach Park. Walk to the trailhead north of the restrooms.

Introductory Notes: Do not try this hike unless you are a confident hiker. The climb to the summit, though short, is extremely steep and the footing is mostly loose volcanic rock.

On the Trail: Across the road from the boat-launching ramp, hala (*Pandanus tectorius*) trees mark the trailhead for the "assault" on Puu Piei (probably, "to peer hill"). Hala is an indigenous tree that grows in coastal areas. It is sometimes called "tourist pineapple," since the fruit resembles a pineapple and is jokingly identified as such by locals for tourists. It has been and continues to be a valuable resource. The hollow trunk of the female tree has been used as a pipe for drainage between taro patches, and the leaves have been used for weaving many items such as baskets, mats and hats—hats being particularly popular with tourists.

The trail climbs the narrow and precipitous ridge to the summit. There is a cable along the ridgeline to assist hikers, but be sure to test it, since it may not be reliable. The view from the summit makes the hike worth the effort. To the east, lovely Kahana (lit., "turning point") Bay lies at your feet and the panorama of the coast is extraordinary. Be equally cautious on your descent.

Kahana Bay from Puu Piei Trail

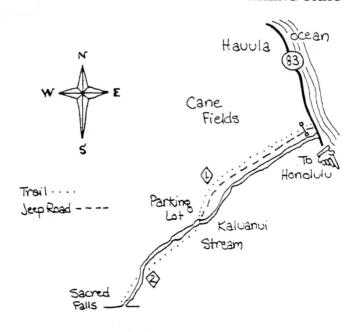

SACRED FALLS

(Hiking Area No. 13)

Rating: Hardy family.

Features: Waterfall, swimming, fruits.

Permission: None.

Hiking Distance & Time: 2.2 miles, 1½ hours.

Driving Instructions: From Honolulu (23 miles, 1¼ hours) drive northwest on H-1, turn right on Route 61 (Pali Highway), then left on Route 83 to a turn-out opposite 53827 Kamehameha Highway (1 mile south of Hauula).

Bus Instructions: From Ala Moana Center take the Honolulu-Kaneohe-Wahiawa bus to Sacred Falls Gift Shop south of Hauula. Cross the highway to the trailhead.

Introductory Notes: Until recently the hike to Sacred Falls was commercialized, and a fee was charged to park at the end of the cane road. Kaliuwaa (lit., "canoe hold" or "canoe leak") is the Hawaiian name for Sacred Falls. Probably the name was changed because "Kaliuwaa" is difficult to pronounce and because "Sacred Falls" sounds more romantic to most tourists. In truth, ancient Hawaiian belief regards the entire valley as sacred to the gods. Legend holds that the pool at the base of the falls is bottomless and leads to another world where a demon lives. The waves in the pool are thought to represent the struggle between the demon and the thrust of the falls, which prevents him from entering this world. Interestingly, another Hawaiian name for the falls and pool is Kaluanua, which literally means "the big pit." To pacify the gods thought to live in the area, believers wrap a stone in a ti leaf and place it along the trail. They believe this act will protect them from falling rocks. Don't miss this hike. Although the trail is usually muddy, it is a fairly easy stroll for the family and offers fruits, picnicking and swimming.

On the Trail: The gate across the cane road which marks the trailhead is 100 feet from the main highway. It is usually locked, so climb over or through the gate and follow the road for 1.2 miles. Ahead, you can see the narrow canyon that contains the falls. The road terminates on a large, flat, grassy area that once served as a parking lot. A rusting sign and a rotting, termite-infested shack are all that remain of commercial enterprise here. Near the shack, the road becomes a trail, which crosses Kaluanua Stream and ascends gently into the canyon. You will find small, red mountain apples, yellow, lemon-sized guava and deep red thimbleberries in great abundance and within in easy reach of the trail.

In addition to the legends mentioned above, this enchanting, lush island paradise is said to be the home of Kamapuaa (lit., "child of a hog"), who was half human and half swine. Near the end of the valley to the left of the trail, you will cross at the base of a dry fall. This is the site, legend recounts, where Kamapuaa turned himself into a giant hog so that his followers could escape a pursuing army by climbing up his back to safety on the ledge above. The deep impression where water only occasionally falls is said to have been made by the weight and size of his body. At this point you might choose to wrap a rock in a ti leaf and place it on the rock fall: no reason to take any chance of being hit by falling rocks, since the valley soon narrows to a 50-feet width.

The falls can be heard crashing to the valley floor and can be seen around the next turn in the trail. The valley walls rise to 1600 feet, but the falls drop only 87 feet. The generous pool at the base is usually muddy and very cold. You might wish to swim or splash in the stream just below the pool. In any event, there is plenty of room for a picnic on the large rocks in this cool, shaded canyon.

Sacred Falls

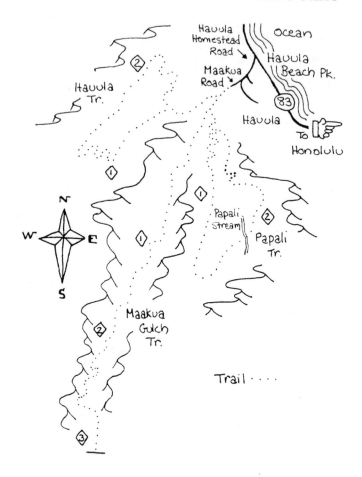

HAUULA

(Hiking Area No. 14)

Rating: See individual hikes.

Features: Views of valley and coastal areas, swimming, waterfall, fruits, native and introduced flora.

Permission: None.

Hiking Distance & Time: See individual hikes.

Driving Instructions: From Honolulu (30 miles, 1¼ hours) drive northwest on H-1, right on Route 61 (Pali Highway), left on Route 83 to Hauula, left on Hauula Homestead Road opposite the north end of Hauula Beach Park for .2 mile and park at the intersection with Maakua Road.

Bus Instructions: From Ala Moana Center take the Honolulu-Kaneohe-Wahiawa bus to Hauula Beach Park. Cross the highway and walk up Hauula Homestead Road to the trailhead.

Introductory Notes: Three relatively easy hikes, camping and swimming await the outdoorsperson in this 20th century Hawaiian community. In Hauula (lit., "abundant hau") you will find old Hawaii mixed with the new. You will find local people surf fishing, throwing a net, "talking stories" and having 3-4 generation ohana ("family") picnics on the beach. There are not many tourists who hike these trails, but you are likely to encounter local school children with their teacher or Boy Scouts with their leader.

On the Trail: Hauula, 2.5 miles loop, 1½ hours, 600-foot gain (trail rating: hardy family)

Walk straight into the woods between the houses on Maakua Road, which becomes a dirt road after the last house. In 200 yards this dirt road becomes mere trail, and 100 yards farther, at a junction, the Maakua Gulch Trail veers left while the less-trod Hauula Trail goes straight ahead. A jeep road turns off to the right shortly before the junction. You pass through some heavy brush, ford a small stream and then switchback up a ridge to where Norfolk Island pines dominate. The fallen needles provide a soft underfooting and make the air aromatic. At midpoint along the ridge, do not take the trail entering on the right but bear left up the ridge. The trail switchbacks up the ridge, traverses Waipilopilo (lit., "smelly water") Gulch, and then ascends along another ridge overlooking Kaipapau (lit., "shallow sea") Valley, from which you have good views of the Koolau Mountain Range and of the east-side coastline and of Hauula. The route then gently slopes and descends to join the initial portion of the trail, on which you retrace your steps.

Maakua Gulch, 3 miles, 3 hours, 1,100-foot gain (trail rating: strenuous)

Walk straight into the woods between the houses on Maakua Road, which becomes a dirt road after the last house. In 200 yards this dirt road becomes mere trail, and 100 yards farther, at a junction, the Maakua Gulch Trail veers left while the less-trod Hauula Trail goes straight ahead. Just 140 yards farther, you pass the start of the Papali Trail on the left.

Maakua Gulch becomes narrower and narrower, and the trail twists and turns along a route which crisscrosses the stream countless times. Be prepared to get wet and to rock-hop throughout the last half of the hike, since the trail is in the streambed there. The narrow canyon and its high, steep walls make this an enchanting hike. Another compensation is the frequent clusters of red mountain apple trees and a good supply of guava trees. The beautiful kukui (*Aleurites moluccana*) tree is common in the gulch. Nicknamed the "candlenut tree," the kukui tree was a valuable resource until the 20th century. Kukui-nut oil was burned for light, the trunk was used to make canoes if the more durable koa tree was not available, and beautiful and popular leis were made of the nuts. To make a lei, each nut must be sanded, filed and polished to a brilliant luster that is acquired from its own oil. Kukui is also the Hawaii State tree. The hike ends at the base of a small cascade—or, if you're an expert scrambler, the base of a small waterfall just above. At the bottom of the waterfall and the bottom of the cascade are pools large enough for a cooling dip.

Papali, 2.5 mile loop, 2 hours, 800-foot gain (trail rating: hardy family)

Walk straight into the woods between the houses on Maakua Road, which becomes a dirt road after the last house. In 200 yards this dirt road becomes mere trail, and 100 yards farther, at a junction, the less-trod Hauula Trail goes straight ahead but your trail veers left. Just 140 yards past the junction, on the left, is the overgrown start of the Papali (lit., "small cliff or slope") Trail. You have to duck and bend to get through the hau (*Hibiscus tiliaceus*) trees at the trailhead. In the wild, this yellow-flowered hibiscus grows twisting and branching along the ground, forming an impenetrable mass of tangled branches. The lightweight hau wood was used for canoe outriggers, fish floats, adze handles and fence posts. Maakua Stream slowly trickles through the hau grove and must be crossed. The trail then climbs sharply along switchbacks, passing concrete slabs that once supported water tanks. The trail heads toward the mountains for about a mile and then turns east and descends into Papali Gulch and crosses tiny Papali Stream. Although you'll share the scenic stream crossing with mosquitoes, pause in this serene place. Civilization seems a long way off. From here, the trail ascends along the ridge, until it rejoins the earlier trail segment near the concrete slabs. In the last mile of the hike you have outstanding views of Hauula town and north to Laie (lit., "'ie leaf") Point.

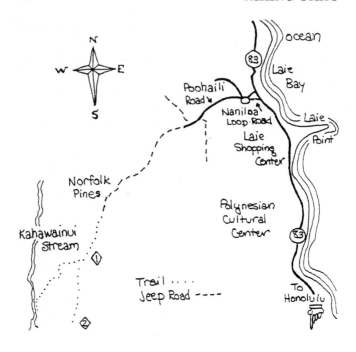

LAIE

(Hiking Area No. 15)

Rating: Strenuous.

Features: Views of east and west sides of the island, native flora, fruits, swimming.

Permission: Secure hiking permit from Zions Securities Corp.

Hiking Distance & Time: 2 miles, 2 hours, 1400-foot gain.

Driving Instructions: From Honolulu (36 miles, 1½ hours) drive northwest on H-1, right on Route 61 (Pali Highway), left on Route 83 to Laie. Go left on Naniloa Loop Road just past the Laie Shopping Center, bear right on Poohaili Road, which shortly becomes a cane road. Drive 2 miles on this road and park by a stand of Norfolk Island Pines. The last mile of the road may be impassable, so that you may have to park off the road and hike to the trailhead.

Bus Instructions: From Ala Moana Center take the Honolulu-Kaneohe-Wahiawa bus to the Laie Shopping Center. Walk north on the highway, left on Naniloa Loop Road, bear right on Poohaili Street, and follow the cane road to the trailhead.

Introductory Notes: Laie attracts thousands of tourists yearly—not to hike in its charming valley, but to visit the Polynesian Cultural Center. A Mormon settlement built over 100 years ago, Laie has, in addition to the cultural center that is owned and operated by the Mormon Church, a branch campus of Brigham Young University and the 'Taj Mahal of the Pacific''— the Mormon Temple.

On the Trail: A stand of Norfolk Island Pines greets the hiker at the end of the dirt road. The trail begins on the mountain side of the grove and contours the side of the main ridge. Strawberry guavas, abundant along the first part of the trail, are a treat to supplement your lunch. This red, walnut-sized fruit can be eaten whole or after removing the small seeds inside. After the first mile, look for a spur trail west (right) which leads into Kahawainui (lit., "great stream") Gulch and along Kahawainui Stream, where a small waterfall and a pool await the hiker. This is a popular wilderness campsite with local people. The main trail continues on the ridge to the summit at 2200 feet, from where the panorama of the north shore can be overwhelming. Indeed, when it is clear, your view extends west to Mokuleia and the Waianae Mountain Range.

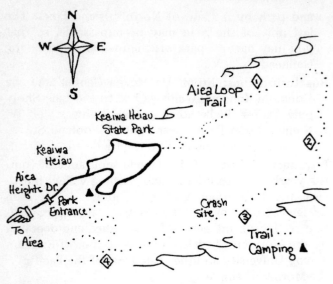

AIEA LOOP

(Hiking Area No. 16)

Rating: Hardy family.

Features: Views of Pearl Harbor, fruits, camping, Keaiwa Heiau.

Permission: Camping permits from Division of State Park.

Hiking Distance & Time: 4.8 miles, 3-hour loop.

Driving Instructions: From Honolulu (12 miles, ½ hour) drive northwest on H-2, right on Aiea off-ramp, and right on Aiea Heights Dr. to end. After entering the park, follow the one-way road to the northeast end of the park and to a sign marking the upper Aiea Loop trailhead.

Bus Instructions: From Ala Moana Center take the Honolulu-Aiea Heights bus to Aiea and to the Kaamilo/Aiea Heights Drive junction. Walk up Aiea Heights Drive to Keaiwa Heiau State Park and to the trailhead.

Introductory Notes: Take time to visit the remains of the heiau (a pre-Christian place of worship) by the park entrance. Keaiwa (lit., "the mystery") Heiau was an ancient healing temple where a priest by the same name was said to have had mysterious healing powers. Keaiwa used the plants grown in the area for medicinal purposes, and instructed novitiates in the art of healing. As is true at so many heiaus in the Islands, little remains of the structures, since they were made mainly of wood and grass. Nevertheless, interpretive displays here provide some information.

Kaeiwa Heiau State Park offers a good family hiking trail, first-class picnic grounds in the forested setting, and a comfortable campground. The Aiea (lit., "Nothocestrum tree") Loop Trail is likely to be crowded on weekends, when local people come to enjoy the park and to hike.

On the Aiea Loop Trail

On the Trail: The first part of the trail snakes along the ridge on a wide and well-maintained path where you can identify thin-barked eucalyptus, symmetrical Norfolk Island pine and ironwood (*Casuarina equisetifolia*), with its long, thin, drooping, dull green needles. Many of these trees are the result of a reforestation program begun by Thomas McGuire in 1928. The shade from the big trees and the trade winds make this part of the hike both cool and pleasurable. Guava is abundant, and with luck you may find ripe strawberry guava, a red, walnut-sized fruit.

The trail makes a sharp right turn at 1.6 miles, where a trail to Koolau Ridge departs eastward, and then follows the ridge above North Halawa (lit., "curve") Stream, from which views of the Koolau Mountains and North Halawa Valley are good. The trail descends through a forest of trees, where you will find some native trees, including koa and ohia lehua. At the 3-mile point, look to the right of the trail for the remains of a C-47 cargo plane that crashed in 1943. Just beyond the crash site, a bridle path leads off to the left to Camp Smith and then the loop trail swings to the right and downhill to cross Aiea Stream. Before crossing the stream, you may choose to stroll along a trail to the left which follows the stream. The Aiea Loop trail crosses the stream and then climbs up to the campground and the lower Aiea Loop trailhead, which is just across the grass below the only toilet building in the camping area.

WAIMANO

(Hiking Area No. 17)

Rating: Difficult.

Features: Views from the Koolau Mountain Range, swimming, native and introduced flora.

Permission: None.

Hiking Distance & Time: 7.1 miles, 4 hours, 1600-foot gain.

Driving Instructions: From Honolulu (14 miles, ½ hour) drive northwest on H-1 to Moanalua Road cutoff (Route 720) and then right on Waimano Home Road (Route 730). There are two trails leading into Waimano Valley, which eventually join. The Lower Ditch Trailhead is reached by driving to the end of Waimano Home Road, to a Division of Forestry sign. From here the route follows a jeep road which becomes a footpath and, after ½ mile, joins the upper trail. The Upper Ditch Trailhead is 2.5 miles up Waimano Home Road from the Kamehameha Highway junction by an irrigation ditch on the north (left) side of the road and a large building on the right. This trail follows the ridgeline above the homestead into the valley for 2½ miles, then joins the Lower Ditch Trail at an irrigation tunnel.

Bus Instructions: From Ala Moana Center take the Honolulu-Pacific Palisades bus to Pearl City Shopping Center (Kamehameha Highway and Waimano Home Road intersection). Transfer to Pearlridge-Pearl City shuttle bus and take to Komo Mai Drive. Walk up Waimano Home Road to the trailhead.

Introductory Notes: Waimano (lit., "many waters") is one of a number of hikes in this book which take

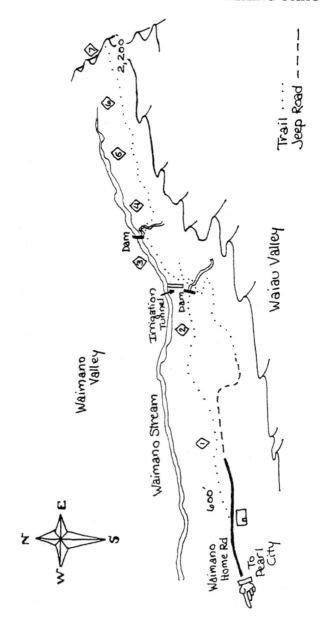

Trail ....
Jeep Road ------

the hiker to viewpoints overlooking the east side of the island from the Koolau Mountain Range. Although this is a much longer hike than the others, there are places to swim and to splash in Waimano Stream. Otherwise the forested area is similar to the other hikes (Hiking Area Nos. 18, 19 and 21).

On the Trail: Whichever approach you take, the first part of the hike is easy. The Upper Ditch Trail follows an irrigation ditch until it reaches a dam and an irrigation tunnel after 2½ miles. At the irrigation tunnel, which is no longer used, the Upper Ditch Trail and the Lower Ditch Trail meet. From here, a single trail switchbacks up to the crest of a ridge overlooking Waimano Stream. For the next mile, the trail follows the ridge above the stream. You can expect to find some generous pools to swim in, if you wish to scramble down the hillside to them. A dam just before the confluence of Waimano Stream and a smaller stream entering from the right mark the point where you start to ascend the ridge which leads to the Koolau summit.

The lower valley contains two of the most noble trees on the island. The kukui (*Aleurites moluccana*), or candlenut tree, a massive tree with maplelike leaves and black, walnut-sized nuts, was one of the most important trees to the island's economy. Kukui-nut oil was burned in stone lamps, the nuts were made into leis and a variety of costume jewelry, and the trunk was used to make canoes. The monkey-pod tree (*Samanea saman*) will commonly grow to 80 feet. It is a symmetrical tree with tiny, delicate, pink tufts when in bloom, and tiny, fernlike leaflets. From the handsome wood, beautiful and highly prized bowls and trays are made. Both trees as well as the familiar hau tree are conspicuous in the valley.

From the last dam, the trail climbs 1600 feet to summit. This is the most difficult part of the trail.

Since the path here is overgrown in places, it is a good idea to wear long pants and a shirt. Periodically, you will have good views of Waimano Valley to the north (left) and of Waiau (lit., "swirling water") Valley to the south (right). However, the highlight of the hike, and the primary reason for making it, is to stand at the summit high above Waihee (lit., "squid liquid") Valley to the east. You will encounter strong winds at the summit. If rain or clouds obstruct your view, be patient, for the winds usually blow the obstruction away quickly.

On the Papali Trail

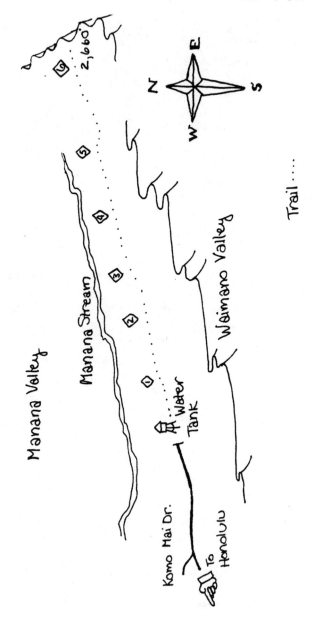

MANANA
(Hiking Area No. 18)

Rating: Difficult.

Features: Views from the Koolau Mountain Range, native and introduced flora.

Permission: None.

Hiking Distance & Time: 6 miles, 4 hours, 1700-foot gain.

Driving Instructions: From Honolulu (15 miles, ½ hour) drive northwest on H-1 to Moanalua Road cutoff (Route 720), then right on Waimano Home Road, for 1.2 miles, and then left on Komo Mai Drive to its end at a Board of Water Supply gate, a water tank and the trailhead.

Bus Instructions: From Ala Moana Center take the Honolulu-Pacific Palisades bus to Pearl City Shopping Center (Kamehameha Highway and Waimano Home Road intersection). Transfer to Pearlridge-Pearl City Shuttle bus and take to Komo Mai Drive. Walk up Komo Mai Drive to trailhead.

Introductory Notes: The Manana Trail is one of a number of trails (Hiking Area Nos. 17, 19 and 21) which take you to peaks atop the Koolau Mountain Range. This trail is little traveled and is overgrown in places, and should be attempted only by skilled hikers. (It is possible to connect with the Waimano Trail by following the cliffs to the south, but the connecting route is very dangerous and not advised.) Rain and mud are frequently encountered in this relatively pristine place. If you are looking for solitude and for the joys as well as the trials present in a rainforest, then Manana will satisfy you.

On the Trail: A pedestrian passageway leads past a water tank which is at the end of the paved road. From here, the Manana Trail climbs 1700 feet to a peak atop the Koolau Range. Eucalyptus, guava and koa trees are abundant along the lower part of the trail, where they are struggling to overcome the ravages of a severe fire in 1972. For your protection, stay on the ridgeline and avoid the side trails, most of which lead to Manana Stream to the north (left) or Waimano Stream to the south. Time permitting, you may wish to hike to Manana Stream for a swim. If so, it would be a good idea to mark your route down so you can follow it back.

In addition to the trees previously noted, look for the majestic sandalwood tree (*Santalum freycinetianum*), with narrow, pointed, shiny leaves. Once an important source of income for the islands, the wood was exported for use in furniture and for its oil and perfume. In fact, China imported so much sandalwood that the Chinese once called Hawaii the "Sandalwood Islands."

A variety of ferns and low scrub dominate the upper part of the trail and seem to reach out to scratch and cut the legs and arms, so protective clothing is well-advised. Strong winds greet the hiker at the summit, but with any luck the air is clear, so that the views into Kaalaea (lit., "the ocherous earth") Valley can be enjoyed. A return via the Waimano Trail is possible for the daring and skilled hiker. The 1-mile hike south to it along the cliffs is extremely dangerous, and a miscalculation could drop the hiker 1500 feet or more to the valley below. Caution is well-advised.

WAHIAWA

(Hiking Area No. 19)

Rating: Strenuous.

Features: Views from the Koolau Mountain Range, native and introduced flora, swimming.

Permission: (1) Secure hiking permit from Division of Forestry. (2) Access permit from U.S. Army, Range Control.

Hiking Distance & Time: 4 miles, 3 hours, 650-foot gain.

Driving Instructions: From Honolulu (22 miles, 1 hour) drive northwest on H-1, then right on H-2 to the end of the freeway just south of Wahiawa. Bear right on Route 80 into Wahiawa and right on California Ave. From the Route 80/California Ave. junction, it is 5 miles to the trailhead. At the end of the Wahiawa Homestead, California Ave. makes a right turn and shortly a left. A few hundred yards down the road on the right there is a gate to the Schofield Barracks East Range. Enter the range land, make a quick left and follow the dirt road for 2 miles until it makes a sharp turn to the right to return to Wahiawa.

Bus Instructions: From Ala Moana Center take the Honolulu-Waihiawa-Kaneohe bus to Wahiawa and to California Ave. Walk up California Ave. to the trailhead, 5 miles.

Introductory Notes: This is the easiest hike to the Koolau Mountain Range crest (See Hiking Area Nos. 17, 18 and 21). However, permission from the military is troublesome to secure. It usually takes three days to get a permit to enter the military reservation,

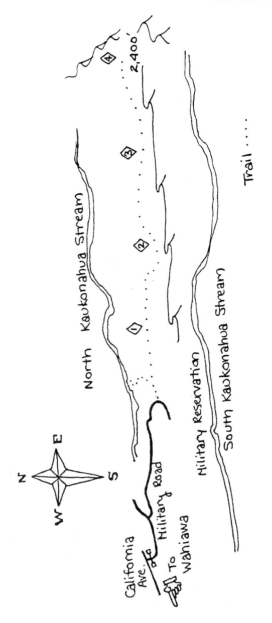

and the trail is usually available to hike only on weekends and on holidays when the range is not in use. Write ahead, and good luck.

On the Trail: The trail begins at the apex of the abrupt right turn on the dirt road. Also known as the Schofield-Waikane Trail, the Wahiawa (lit., "milkfish place") Trail parallels the military-reservation boundary and travels between the north and south forks of Kaikonahua (probably, "fat place") Stream. This 33-mile-long stream is the longest in the State. Damage caused by the 1970 Kipapa (lit., "placed prone") fire is evident along the first part of the trail. A short distance from the trailhead (.4 mile) a trail descends north (left) to the north fork of Kaikonahua Stream, along which you can find a number of swimming holes. The stream is 400 vertical feet and .4 miles below the main trail but is worth a side trip to visit and to swim in.

Ohia lehua, ohia ha, naupaka and olapa are a few of the native plants found along the trail. The olapa (*Cheirodendron gaudichaudii*) is a native mountain tree from which early Hawaiians cut poles. They put a sticky, gummy substance on one end of a pole to catch birds for their feathers. Bird feathers were highly prized, particularly by Hawaiian royalty for making garments. Another tree, ohia ha (*Syzygium sandwicense*) played an important part in early Hawaii. The hard and durable reddish wood was used for house timbers and paddles. It is a large tree whose reddish-brown, smooth bark yielded a black dye.

The trail follows the ridgeline, dipping between saddles until it reaches the summit at 2400 feet. From high above the floor of Kahana Valley 1500 feet below, the views of the east side are superb. However, as is usually the condition all along the Koolau pali, strong winds buffet the hiker here.

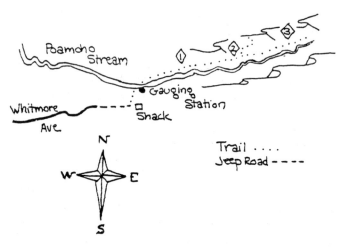

POAMOHO VALLEY

(Hiking Area No. 20)

Rating: Hardy family.

Features: Introduced and native flora, swimming.

Permission: (1) Hiking permit from Division of Forestry. (2) Access permit from U.S. Army, Range Control.

Hiking Distance & Time: 3 miles, 2 hours, 1000-foot gain.

Driving Instructions: From Honolulu (22 miles, 1 hour) drive northwest on H-1, then right on H-2 to the end of the freeway just south of Wahiawa. Bear right on Route 80 into Wahiawa and right on Whitmore Ave. (Route 804) to its end, then continue on a jeep road to its end by an abandoned shack.

Bus Instructions: From Ala Moana Center take the Honolulu-Wahiawa-Kaneohe bus to Wahiawa and to California Ave. Walk north on Kamehameha Highway and then right on Whitmore Ave 2 miles to the trailhead.

Introductory Notes: The hike into Poamoho Valley is rough and wet. There is no trail, so the hiker must follow the stream and do a lot of rock-hopping. However, that is the joy of the hike. There are numerous swimming holes and places to splash and to picnic.

On the Trail: The trail descends a short distance to the north (left) of the shack, and joins Poamoho Stream near a gauging station. Since the valley was once the site of a plantation arboretum, the hiker is treated to a great variety of introduced and native flora. The former includes eucalyptus and paper bark and the latter includes koa and kukui trees. Paper bark (*Melaleuca leucadendra*) is an interesting tree, characterized by a bark that peels off in sheets that are very much like paper.

The valley alternately narrows and widens as we hike east. After 2 miles, look for a spur trail which leads north (left) up the cliffs to join the Poamoho Ridge Trail. From this junction, you may choose to hike the Poamoho Ridge Trail to the ridge along the Koolau Range, which is 1.5 miles and 1000 feet of elevation gain distant. If not, the stream trail continues into the valley for another mile. After that, large boulders and thick vegetation make hiking difficult and dangerous.

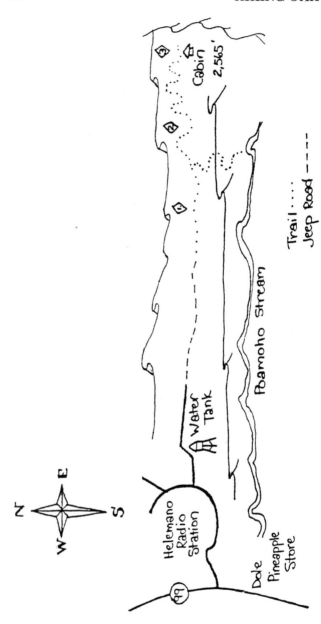

POAMOHO RIDGE
(Hiking Area No. 21)

Rating: Strenuous.

Features: Views from the Koolau Mountain Range, native and introduced flora, camping.

Permission: (1) Hiking, camping and shelter-use permit from Division of Forestry. (2) Access permit from U.S. Army, Range Control. (3) Access permit from Dole Pineapple Co. (4) Access permit from Waialua Sugar Company.

Hiking Distance & Time: 3.4 miles, 3 hours, 800-foot gain.

Driving Instructions: From Honolulu (28 miles 1½ hours) drive northwest on H-1, then right on H-2 to the end of the freeway just south of Wahiawa. Bear left on Route 99 to the Dole Pineapple stand north of Wahiawa. Turn right on a dirt road just past the stand and follow it to the trailhead (5.5 miles). First you circle to the right around the U.S. Army Helemano Radio Station and then turn right past a water tank through a pineapple field and then through a cane field to the Forest Reserve boundary. The last 2 miles are on a rough jeep road along the ridge to the trailhead.

Bus Instructions: From Ala Moana Center take the Honolulu-Wahiawa-Kaneohe bus to the Dole Pineapple stand north of Wahiawa. Walk north to the road past the stand and follow the road to the trailhead, 5.5 miles.

Introductory Notes: Securing permission for this hike is complicated and takes a few days. Additionally, the trail is ordinarily open only on weekends and on holidays. Time permitting, make the effort, for this is a delightful hike over some little-traveled terrain.

On the Trail: The trail begins east of the parking area at the end of the road and follows the main ridge until it reaches the summit of the Koolau Mountain Range. Avoid the hunting trails that lead off the main ridge, for many simply lead into the brush or loop to rejoin the ridge trail. At the 1.5-mile point, you can hike south (right) a short distance down into the valley to Poamoho Stream. There are a few swimming spots and places to picnic along it. A number of native trees can be identified along the ridge and in the valley, such as ohia, koa and kawau. The kawau (*Byronia sandwicensis*), or Hawaiian holly tree, is distinguised by grayish-yellow wood, white blossoms and black berries.

A surprise awaits the hiker at the summit: the viewpoint here has a generous, flat, grassy area. From its east end one has magnificent views of Punaluu Valley and Kahana Valley to the southeast. In the absence of rain or fog, the summit is a delightful place to find solitude as well as a panorama of the island. A short hike (0.2 mile) south (right) along the summit trail leads to an overnight Forest Reserve cabin. Although the shelter does not provide any amenities, the alternative to spending overnight in it is to tent on the wet ground and to endure nightly rains and wind.

DUPONT

(Hiking Area No. 22)

Rating: Difficult (and dangerous).

Features: Views from the highest point on Oahu (4,025 feet), forest and pasture land, native flora.

Permission: (1) Hiking permit from Division of Forestry. (2) Liability waiver from Waialua Sugar Company.

Hiking Distance & Time: 4 miles, 5 hours, 3800-foot gain.

Driving Instructions: From Honolulu (30 miles, 1½ hours) drive northwest on H-1, then right on H-2 to end of freeway (completed to Wahiawa at time of writing). Continue on Route 99, then bear left on Route 803. At a traffic circle, take Route 930 west to Waialua and to Waialua High School. Go left on a cane road just past the school. Drive 1.5 miles up road and park by the second gate.

Bus Instructions: From Ala Moana Center take the Honolulu-Wahiawa-Kaneohe bus to Wahiawa and to California Ave. Transfer to the Waialua-Haleiwa bus and take it to the Goodale Ave./Farrington Highway junction in Waialua. Walk or hitchhike west on the highway to the trailhead.

Introductory Notes: Mt. Kaala (probably, "to hurl stones with a sling") is noteworthy for at least two reasons; it is the highest point on Oahu and the ascent of it is the most difficult hike on the island. The last mile of the hike is very dangerous, and requires skill and a stout heart. Parts of this trail require the hiker to scramble, climb and crawl along narrow ledges with a 2000-foot drop into the valley below. (Ropes have been placed to aid hikers in the most difficult

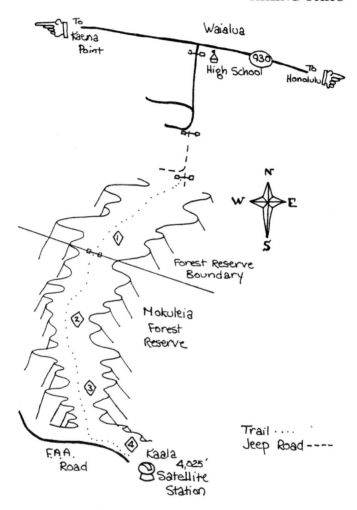

places.) If heights are a problem for you, DO NOT
attempt this hike. This is not a hike for timid people!
You can reach the summit via a longer route on roads.

On the Trail: The Dupont Trail begins beyond the
second gate, where the road makes a right turn. Proceed straight ahead on the jeep road a short distance

until you reach a gate that secures the pasture land, where the jeep road turns right. From here, Mt. Kaala, distinguished by the white, domed radio and radar installations, is to your front-left while Kau- pakuhale (lit., "house ridgepole or roof") Ridge is to your front-right. You must hike cross-county up Kaupakuhale Ridge. There is no trail until you reach the Forest Reserve boundary 1.3 miles distant. There- fore, you should walk toward the ridge through the pasture land and over a few small hills. What appear to be trails are simply cattle contours, which will lead you in circles if you follow them. A fence and a lock- ed gate on the ridge mark the beginning of the foot trail through the Mokuleia (lit., "isle of abundance") Forest Reserve.

Trailhead, Dupont Trail

The difference between the pasture and the forest is apparent. The forest part of the trail passes through heavy foliage, which periodically obscures the trail. However, the ridge begins to narrow considerably, and the danger does not lie in losing the trail but rather in stumbling or sliding off the ridge. A variety of native plants is evident in the forest. Ohia, with its bright red flowers, and hapuu (*Cibotium chamissoi*), or Hawaiian tree fern, are plentiful. The most notable use of the tree fern has been the carving of tikis (carved representation of ancestors) from the trunk. In times of famine, the stems and the core of the trunk have been used for food.

As you ascend, the ridge will alternately narrow and widen. Be cautious and alert, particularly in those places where the footing is composed of loose and brittle volcanic rock. Pause frequently to study the trail ahead and to enjoy the views of the north side of the island and of the deep and startling valleys and gulches on each side of the ridge. The last 1 mile climbs 1800 feet and is the most dangerous part of the hike. Ropes have been placed at the most difficult and the narrowest parts of the ridge. BE CERTAIN to test these ropes to determine whether they will support your weight. Indeed, you may wish to pause and consider returning down the trail rather than risking the difficult ascent ahead.

Abruptly, the trail meets a paved road, which will take you to the summit ¼ mile away. Federal officials do not welcome visitors to the radio and radar facilities at the summit, as numerous "no trespassing" signs attest. Mt. Kaala presides over the island at 4,025 feet. The summit is a mile-wide plateau containing a montane bog which has been considerably altered by building over the years. On a clear day, the views of the island, particularly those to the west, are overwhelming. Makaha Valley lies at your feet, and

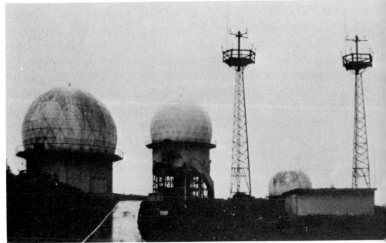

Military installations on Mt. Kaala

the sweep of the coastline to Kaena Point is sufficient reward for your efforts.

From the summit you may choose to follow the road instead of returning via the trail. It is 8.3 miles to Farrington Highway. If you're lucky, you might get a ride in one of the service vehicles or with the personnel who work at the summit installation. Hawaiian raspberries (*Rubus hawaiiensis*) are abundant along the road, and although the dark berries are edible, they can be rather bitter.

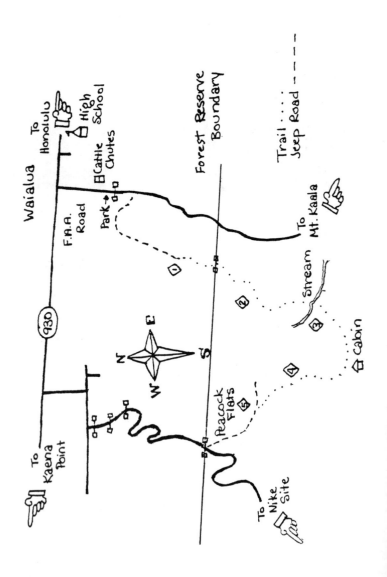

MOKULEIA

(Hiking Area No. 23)

Rating: Strenuous.

Features: Views of central Oahu, forest and pasture land, native flora.

Permission: (1) Hiking and camping permit from Division of Forestry. (2) Liability waiver from Waialua Sugar Company.

Hiking Distance & Time: 5.4 miles, 5 hours, 1,900-foot gain.

Driving Instructions: From Honolulu (32 miles, 1½ hours) drive northwest on H-1, then right on H-2 to end of freeway (completed to Wahiawa at time of writing). Continue on Route 99, then bear left on Route 803. At a traffic circle, take Route 930 west to Waialua and Waialua High School. Turn left 1.3 miles after school on Mt. Kaala Rd., which is lined with telephone poles. Drive 1 mile to the FAA (Federal Aviation Administration) gate which prohibits further civilian travel. Park off the road and away from the cattle chutes.

Bus Instructions: From Ala Moana Center take the Honolulu-Wahiawa-Kaneohe bus to Wahiawa and to California Ave. Transfer to the Waialua-Haleiwa bus and take it to the Goodale Ave./Farrington Highway junction in Waialua. Walk or hitchhike west on the highway to the trailhead.

Introductory Notes: This vigorous hike traverses a beautiful forested area and ends on Peacock Flats, a delightful primitive camping site. As an alternative, you could drive to Peacock Flats (see Hiking Area

No. 24 for permission, keys to the gate, and the route), camp, and hike this trail to the FAA Road.

On the Trail: Walk around the gate and follow the road for about .3 mile, to where a jeep road enters on the right. Hike the jeep road as it contours along the ridge to a point where the road becomes a footpath that leads into the mountains. This trail ascends the ridge to 1450 feet elevation and the Mokuleia Forest Reserve boundary gate. Throughout the forest a number of native trees can be identified. The ohia lehua, with its bright red flowers, is common. Look for the "Hawaiian olive," which is a common tree in the lower forest. The purple fruit of the olopua (*Osmanthus sandwicensis*), which is not edible, resembles ripe olives. The yellowish-brown wood with black streaks is very hard and was once used for adze handles and to shape fish hooks. The papala (*Charpentiera obovata*) tree was used as the Hawaiian version of fireworks. The wood of this tree with tiny, reddish flowers is so light and fibrous that when it is dry, it will burn like paper. Pieces of wood were lit and thrown into the air where the wind currents were strong, and the lighted sticks stayed afloat until they burned out.

Once in the forest, there are numerous places to pause in the shade and to enjoy the views of the lowland area between the Koolau and the Waianae mountain ranges and of the ocean along the north shore. Mt. Kaala presides over the Waianae Mountain Range to the southeast (front-left). The radio/radar facility at the summit is conspicuous along most of the trail. The trail reaches and crosses a small stream at 2100 feet elevation, at the 3-mile point. Although the water is tempting, it is advisable not to drink it without boiling it because the stream is used by feral goats and pigs. A short distance beyond the stream is a large old cabin situated just below the summit ridge.

Outstanding views of Makua (lit, "parents") Valley on the west side can be had from the ridge. From the cabin, the trail leads north and descends 500 vertical feet to a jeep road on Peacock Flats. Follow the jeep road northwest (left) to a paved road, which goes to an abandoned Nike missile site. East of the junction of the jeep road and the paved road, on Peacock Flats, is a primitive campsite in a grove of eucalyptus trees. Although it can be rainy here, it is nevertheless a good place to camp and to use as a base for hiking in the Forest Reserve.

Waianae Range above Mokuleia Trail

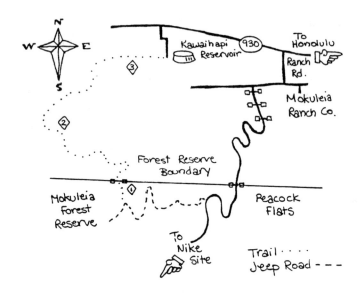

PEACOCK FLATS

(Hiking Area No. 24)

Rating: Hardy family.

Features: Views of central Oahu, forest and pasture land, camping.

Permission: (1) Hiking and camping permit from Division of Forestry. (2) Liability waiver from Mokuleia Ranch and Land Co., Mokuleia, Oahu, 96786 (Phone 637-4241).

Hiking Distance & Time: 3.5 miles, 3 hours, 1600-foot gain.

Driving Instructions: From Honolulu (40 miles, 2½ hours) drive northwest on H-1, then right on H-2 to end of freeway (completed to Wahiawa at time of writing). Continue on Route 99, then bear left on Route 803. At a traffic circle, take Route 930 west to Waialua. Turn left (south) at a sign "Mokuleia Ranch and Land Co." for .6 miles to ranch office. Secure permits and gate key. Follow the ranch road (see map) for .7 mile to a green, locked gate on the left across a paved road. Unlock it and pass through it and two more gates before reaching the Mokuleia Forest Reserve boundary at a fourth gate. Peacock Flats is past the fourth gate and the Peacock Flats trailhead is .5 miles further up this paved road at the Mokuleia firebreak road on the right. Park off the road on the turnout.

Bus Instructions: From Ala Moana Center take the Honolulu-Wahiawa-Kaneohe bus to Wahiawa and to California Ave. Transfer to the Waialua-Haleiwa bus and take it to the Goodale Ave./Farrington Highway junction in Waialua. Walk or hitchhike west on the highway to the trailhead.

Introductory Notes: Peacock Flats and the Mokuleia Forest are a joy for hiking and camping for the entire family. Although you may camp along the trail, a primitive campsite in a eucalyptus grove on Peacock Flats is a good place to make a base camp. To reach the other end of the Peacock Flats Trail, turn left off Farrington Highway (Route 930) on a dirt road 1000 feet before Dillingham airfield. The road leads past a pumping station to Kawaihapai Reservoir, and the Peacock Flats Trail begins west of the reservoir.

On the Trail: Follow the Mokuleia firebreak road as it contours west. The road is heavily rutted and may be wet and muddy. It is well-used by hunters, whom you are likely to meet in their four-wheel-drive vehicles. The area from the paved road to Kaena Point on the coast is a popular hunting area. In fact, two Division of Forestry trails, Kuaokala and Kealia, west of the Peacock Flats Trail, are reserved for hunters.

At the 1-mile point, the Peacock Flats foot trail begins north (right) of the road and shortly leaves the Forest Reserve. From a 1600-foot perch overlooking the north side, the trail makes a gentle descent

through pasture land to the Kawaihapai (lit., "the
carried water") Reservoir. A number of birds can be
seen busily foraging for food. Both male and female
cardinals (*Cardinalis cardinalis*) are common. The
male is bright red, while the female is reddish brown.
From the reservoir it is .8 mile to the main highway,
Route 930.

View northward from Mokuleia Trail

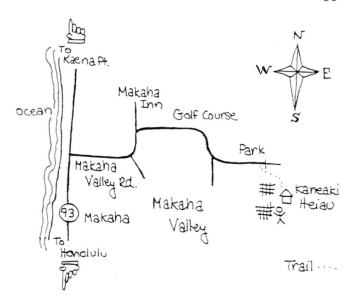

KANEAKI HEIAU

(Hiking Area No. 25)

Rating: Family.

Features: Kaneaki Heiau, fruits, native and introduced flora.

Permission: Access from 11 a.m. to 1 p.m. Tuesday-Sunday.

Hiking Distance & Time: .5 mile, ½ hour.

Driving Instructions: From Honolulu (36 miles, 1½ hours) drive northwest on H-1, which becomes Route 93 when the freeway ends. In Makaha, go right on Makaha Valley Road. After turning left toward the Makaha Inn, take a right on a paved road which cuts through the golf course for .7 mile. Follow the road as it turns right, then take the first left to the end (.7 mile). Park off the road on the left.

Bus Instructions: From Ala Moana Center take the Honolulu-Makaha bus to Makaha. Walk up Makaha Valley Road or take the Makaha Inn shuttle to the paved road leading to the golf course and to the trailhead.

Introductory Notes: If you are on the leeward side of the island, it is worth a visit. Today, Makaha (lit., "fierce") Valley is rapidly developing into a tourist center. Historically, Makaha was noted for robbers and for cannibals, although there is some question whether people there really cannibalized.

On the Trail: From the parking area follow the road for about 50 feet to a footpath on the right which leads directly to the heiau, a pre-Christian place of worship. Kaneaki, restored in 1969-70, is one of the best-preserved heiaus on Oahu. Built in the 13th Century, Kaneaki was first used as a temple for agricultural worship. It later became a temple to the god of war. A number of structures and ceremonial sites have been reconstructed, identified by interpretive signs. For example, there are the hale-pahu, or drum house, and the hale-mana, or house of spiritual power, from which the Kahunas ("priests") received power. There are also a lele ("altar"), a number of kikis ("images") and two anuus, or towers of worship. A stroll through the heiau provides some insight into the role played by these important religious and cultural places.

An array of native and introduced flora enhances the beauty of the heiau and of Makaha (lit., "fierce") Valley. Two fruits are readily available. Papaya (*Carica papaya*) is found growing in clusters at the bases of umbrellalike leaves. Yellow when ripe, the sweet papaya fruit is usually the size of a squash and is a favorite of visitors and locals. Guava is also plentiful, so choose the ripest of these yellow, lemon-sized fruits. A shower of color is provided by red and white hibiscus—the Hawaii state flower—crotons, with their multicolored leaves, and the striking heliconia (*Heliconia humilis*), or lobster claw. The bright red bracts of this flower, which resemble the claw of a boiled lobster, are used by practitioners of ikebana— flower arranging. Shade in this area is provided by towering kukui trees.

Tiki at Kaneaki Heiau

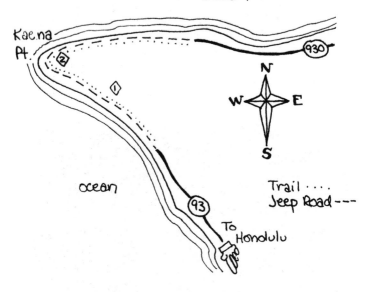

KAENA POINT

(Hiking Area No. 26)

Rating: Hardy family.

Features: Views of coastal area, tidepools, swimming.

Permission: None.

Hiking Distance & Time: 2 miles, 1½ hours.

Driving Instructions: From Honolulu (42 miles, 2 hours) drive northwest on H-2, which becomes Route 93 when the freeway ends. Drive past Makua town to the end of the paved road as far as you dare. Large holes and dirt barriers make passage difficult even for four-wheel-drive vehicles.

Bus Instructions: From Ala Moana Center take the Honolulu-Makaha bus to the end of the line near the surfing beach north of Makaha. Walk north to the end of the road and to the trailhead.

Introductory Notes: The trade winds and the ocean offer some relief along this hot and dusty hike. Instead of the west shore, you may choose to hike to Kaena Point along the north shore, if you are camping at Mokuleia or touring in that area.

On the Trail: The trail begins from the point to which you dare to drive. You may hike the road, which follows the coastline, or walk along the shore, where you can splash to cool off and can investigate tidepools and the collection of debris washed onto shore. You are likely to find local people fishing, snorkeling and throwing nets. Visit with them and check out their catch. I have never known a local to be "skunked" fishing. The thorny kiawe tree dominates the area, but its growth is usually stunted due to the lack of water.

Legends abound concerning Kaena (lit., "the heat") Point. One legend claims that the demigod Maui cast his giant hook from here to the island of Kauai in an attempt to join Oahu and Kauai. He hooked Kauai and gave a tremendous tug. A rock broke off and landed at his feet, while his hook sailed over his head and landed in Palolo Valley, making Kaau Crater (see Hiking Area No. 9). The farther of two islets off Kaena Point, Pohaku-o-Kauai (lit., "rock of Kauai"), is said to be the rock that was broken off from Kauai by Maui. Another legend regarding this islet tells of Haupu, a great warrior from Kauai who had a short temper. It seems that the noise from a hukilau, or fishing party, being held on the point so disturbed Haupu that he hurled this huge rock, killing many people. There is no legend regarding the other, somewhat smaller islet, named Pohaku-o-Oahu (lit., "rock of Oahu"), which is closer to shore.

Legend aside, Kaena Point was an important place in pre-Christian religious belief. It was thought to be the place where the souls of Hawaiian dead began

their journey to Kahiki—the immortal land of their
ancestors. A white rock about .4 mile offshore was
believed to be the exact point from which the soul
made its leap to the Other World. The rock is called
Leina Kauhane (lit., "leaping place of ghosts").

Coast near Kaena Point

Appendix

Division of State Parks
1151 Punchbowl St.
Room 310
Honolulu, Oahu 96813
Tel. 548-7455

1. camping permit for state park
2. hiking permit for Diamond Head

Zions Securities Corp.
Laie Shopping Center
55-510 Kamehameha Highway
Laie, Oahu 96762
Tel. 293-9201

1. hiking permit for Laie (No. 15)

Division of Forestry
2135 Makiki Heights Dr.
Honolulu, Oahu 96822
Tel. 946-2004

1. hiking permits
2. camping and shelter use permits

U.S. Army, Range Control
Schofield Barracks, Oahu 96786
Tel. 655-0033

1. access permit

Dole Pineapple Co.
Tel. 621-5052

1. access permit

Waialua Sugar Co.
Waialua, Oahu 96786
Tel. 637-4436

1. access permit

Mokuleia Ranch and Land Co.
Mokuleia, Oahu 96786
Tel. 637-4241

1. access permit

Department of Parks and
    Recreation
Honolulu Municipal Building
Honolulu, Oahu 96813
Tel. 955-3711

1. camping permits

OR from Satellite City Halls:

Kaneohe
46-018 Kam Hwy.
Kaneohe, Oahu 96744
Tel. 235-4571

Kailua
302 Kuulei Rd.
Kailua, Oahu 96734
Tel. 261-8575

Wahiawa
830 California Ave.
Wahiawa, Oahu 96786
Tel. 621-0791

Waianae
85-555 Farrington Hwy.
Waianae, Oahu 96792
Tel. 696-6371

Beretania
1290 Aala St.
Honolulu, Oahu 96817
Tel. 523-2405

Kalihi
1865 Kam IV Road
Honolulu, Oahu 96819
Tel. 847-4688

Hawaii Kai
2nd Floor
Koko Marina Shopping Center.
Honolulu, Oahu 96825
Tel. 395-4418

Ewa
91-923 Ft. Weaver Road
Ewa Beach, Oahu 96706
Tel. 689-7914

Waipahu
Waipahu Shopping Plaza
Tel. 671-5638

Hauula
Hauula Kai Shopping Center
54-316 Kam Hwy.
Tel. 293-8551

Index